The Religion of White Supremacy in the United States

Religion and Race

Series Editors: Monica R. Miller, Lehigh University
Anthony B. Pinn, Rice University

The local/global connections between religion and race are complex, interrelated, ever changing, and undeniable. *Religion and Race* bridges these multifaceted dimensions within a context of cultural complexity and increasing sociopolitical realities of identity and difference in a multidisciplinary manner that offers a strong platform for scholars to examine the relationship between religion and race. This series is committed to a range of social science and humanities approaches, including media studies, cultural studies, and feminist and queer methods, and welcomes books from a variety of global and cultural contexts from the modern period to projects considering the dynamics of the "postmodern" context. While the series will privilege monographs, it will also consider exceptional edited volumes. *Religion and Race seeks* to impact historical and contemporary cultural and sociopolitical conversations through comparative scholarly examinations that tap the similarities and distinctions of race across geographies within the context of a variety of religious traditions and practices.

Titles in the Series

The Religion of White Supremacy in the United States

Eric Weed

LEXINGTON BOOKS
Lanham • Boulder • New York • London

Published by Lexington Books
An imprint of The Rowman & Littlefield Publishing Group, Inc.
4501 Forbes Boulevard, Suite 200, Lanham, Maryland 20706
www.rowman.com

Unit A, Whitacre Mews, 26-34 Stannary Street, London SE11 4AB

British Library Cataloguing in Publication Information Available
The hardback edition of this book was previously catalogued by the Library of Congress
as follows:

Library of Congress Cataloging-in-Publication Data

Names: Weed, Eric Arden, author.
Title: The religion of white supremacy in the United States / Eric Weed.
Description: Lanham : Lexington, 2017. | Series: Religion and race | Includes
  bibliographical references and index.
Identifiers: LCCN 2017032855 (print) | LCCN 2017027969 (ebook) | ISBN
  9781498538763 (Electronic) | ISBN 9781498538756 (cloth : alk. paper) |
  ISBN 9781498538770 (pbk. : alk. paper)
Subjects: LCSH: Whites—Race identity—United States. | White supremacy
  movements—United States—Religious aspects. | Protestantism—United
  States—History. | Racism—Religious aspects—Christianity—History.
Classification: LCC E184.A1 (print) | LCC E184.A1 W338 2017 (ebook) | DDC
  305.80973—dc23
LC record available at https://lccn.loc.gov/2017032855

ISBN 978-1-4985-3875-6 (cloth : alk. paper)
ISBN 978-1-4985-3877-0 (pbk. : alk. paper)
ISBN 978-1-4985-3876-3 (electronic)

Printed in the United States of America

Dedicated to Elizabeth and Katerina

Contents

Foreword

Sparked by troubling and graphic performances of whiteness during the "Age of Obama," Eric Weed turned his attention away from the dynamics of racial disregard elsewhere in the world and began to interrogate the theological platform supporting the religion of white supremacy at home, in the United States. "When I saw the workings of white supremacy in the past and present," writes Weed, "I saw myself." In making this statement, Weed acknowledges the manner in which the deep (i.e. religious) workings of whiteness have informed historically the workings of the United States, while being arranged and performed in such a way as to allow whites to claim ignorance. In other words, "it's a siren song that blinds all whites," as he puts it. His aim, in this book, is to expose this dilemma and interrogate its religious-theological underpinning and rationale.

The Religion of White Supremacy in the United States is an important and timely addition to the growing scholarly literature (e.g. Christopher Driscoll and George Yancy) decoding the religiosity of whiteness—its framing of a deep and abiding grammar and vocabulary of meaning performed through coded claims to social-cultural dominance. Using a methodology he labels "theo-historical," Weed presents and critiques the graphic workings of a religion of white supremacy as it produces images of divinity (e.g. Sallman's "Head of Christ") that shape the aesthetics of humanity at its best, and sanction sociopolitical and economic codes that justify the disadvantaging of those who aren't authorized to claim whiteness. Put differently, the normalization of whiteness in a way that accounts for a particular metaphysics of life geared toward the well-being of a particular group against "darker" neighbors is, according to Weed, *the* American experience. Through this approach, Weed exposes readers to the manner in which the United States can be understood through racial strategies as framework for historically situated exceptionalism that produces and is produced by symbol systems and signifiers of whiteness. Furthermore, as Weed notes, the markers of whiteness (i.e. cultural and physiological claims) are inseparable from markers of "ultimacy" understood in terms of the historical "look" of thick meaning, which already and always positions one population—whites—over all others.

Responses to the presidency of Obama made explicit such workings of whiteness in that the "naturalness" of white supremacy took a blow, and the various adjustments necessary to maintain its correctness took place in unusually transparent ways concluding with the election of Donald Trump. Readers are encouraged by Weed to think this through in light of the theo-historical coding of his claim to make "America great again" as a statement about the re-assurgency of whiteness as the marker of dominance and chosenness.

This important book doesn't simply present and analyze whiteness so conceived. Rather, it uses this presentation of the religion of whiteness as a call to take seriously the enduring impact of race, and to speak about the workings of whiteness in ways that cut its strength to determine public life. That is to say, Weed's goal is to further foster conversation concerning the workings of whiteness, and to give this conversation greater space and urgency. By means of this intervention, *The Religion of White Supremacy in the United States* offers both scholars and general readers an important and creative way of viewing the ongoing significance of whiteness and its relationship to U.S. structures of deep meaning. The book's aims and findings make it an ideal addition to the Lexington series on *Race and Religion*. We are delighted to make it available to you.

Anthony B. Pinn
Rice University

Preface

The idea of white supremacy as a religion will be seen as an interesting argument by my white compatriots in the study of religion. I have received comments by white scholars trying to seem anywhere from fascinated to puzzled about why I spent the very beginning of my career on such a project. I have had whites assume that the religion of white supremacy meant my work focused on neo-Nazis or the Ku Klux Klan. Each response has one element in common: all white responses deflect the idea of being a faithful member of white supremacy away from themselves. Much like the white scholars described at the beginning of George Yancy's *Look! A White*, no one wants to consider themselves as a coreligionist with Nathan Bedford Forrest, Father Charles Coughlin, or David Duke. To be honest, I have had the same thoughts even though I committed myself to the deconstruction of this theology.

When I discuss this project with minority scholars, the response turns from surprise or puzzlement to one of commonsense agreement. The question becomes, why do whites seem surprised while nonwhite scholars do not? The simple answer is the problem of whiteness. As a beneficiary of whiteness, I can step back from the messiness of race at any moment. I can choose to engage or not. I can deflect and say "not I." I can point to racism as a problem of real racists and claim my innocence at any moment. And yet, this very deflection from myself confirms my place within the congregation of white supremacy.

I did not start graduate school considering racism and white supremacy in the American context. I spent seven years focusing my attention on the Holocaust and how good Christians in Germany could be mesmerized by the rhetoric of Adolf Hitler and the Nazi Party. I was content in studying the racist past of another country. It allowed me to study part of the human psyche without ever questioning my own part in the history of suffering. The election of President Barack Obama forced me to turn my gaze to the United States and, subsequently, myself. What I thought was the racist past came alive right in front of me. By the spring of 2010, I knew I could no longer detach my research from my life. I started this move by looking at the Tulsa Race Riot of 1921. The similarities between Tulsa and *Kristallnacht* shook me. Reading about Tulsa led me to reading about lynching, which led to reading about the Klan. Each piece kept the racist past at a safe distance from my own life.

The safety of the past eluded me with the unrelenting questions in the public discourse about the citizenship of President Obama. I could no longer hide in the safety of history. There was no separating the study of extraordinary racism from the continued assaults against the personhood of Obama. I could not shake questions about what made the president less American than myself. *The Religion of White Supremacy in the United States* is a direct result of this lingering question. I could no longer detach myself from my work. When I saw the workings of white supremacy in the past and present, I saw myself. In this way, *The Religion of White Supremacy in the United States* unpacks how white supremacy haunts the United States, but also how it's a siren song that blinds all whites.

Before acknowledging those who helped make this book possible, it is necessary to make a brief comment about the cover. The reader will notice I refer several times to Warner Sallman's *Head of Christ* when pointing to the idea of the white Christ. It was my hope to solidify this connection through using *Head of Christ* as the cover image of the book. As with using any other copyrighted image, I enquired about receiving permission from the copyright holder. I did not receive permission to use *Head of Christ* for this book. The press declining permission to use the painting is its choice. I respectfully accept the decision. The reason for this side note is the rationale used to deny the request. The reasoning for denying my request was based on Sallman's belief in his images being true depictions of Christ. As such, *Head of Christ* is a "divinely inspired" image of the historical Christ. The copyright holder's justification based on Sallman's own beliefs solidifies the troubled legacy of whiteness in U.S. culture. The reasoning for denying the request confirms the ubiquitous nature and the importance of *Head of Christ* to the argument advanced in these pages. Sallman himself saw this painting as a divinely inspired image of Christ that was spiritually significant. On this point, I agree with Sallman and the copyright holder; and yet, denying that *Head of Christ*'s possible unintended consequences as a cultural piece that affirms whiteness is also troubling.

My journey to this point includes naming more people than could be reasonably mentioned. Suffice it to say, I must thank my mentors throughout the years. As an undergraduate student at Capital University, Jacqueline Bussie took an interest in helping me first question and then to better understand my own faith. She showed me that faith and action could not be separated in a meaningful life. It is our conversations that led me to question the role of the Christian faith in the Holocaust. Without our moments together, I would not have pursued theological education. After my first year in seminary at The Lutheran Theological Seminary in Philadelphia (LTSP), I had the great opportunity of working with Victoria J. Barnett and the wonderful people at The Jack, Joseph and Morten Mandel Center for Advanced Holocaust Studies at the United States Holocaust Memorial Museum in Washington, D.C. The next summer I returned as a Dorot Summer Graduate Research Fellow. These two summers provided me an intensive setting to learn to be a scholar. As of right now, my work has moved on from studying the Holocaust, but these two summers have left their mark on my identity as a scholar.

While studying at LTSP, I met Stephen G. Ray Jr., who molded me into the scholar I am today. He has guided me through some of best times of my life and some of the hardest. In the ten years we have worked together, he has become more of a father figure than an academic advisor. He was there in moments of panic as I prepared for doctoral exams and pushed me when the dissertation seemed like an impossible task.

While finishing my doctorate, I met some scholars who will always hold a place in my work. Edward J. Blum and Angela D. Sims took time out of their own busy academic portfolios to give me a place to think and discuss my work.

I must thank Sarah Craig at Lexington Books for seeing promise in this work and helping me transform the book to what it is today. A young scholar could not ask for a better first editor. In addition to Sarah, I must thank Anthony B. Pinn and Monica Miller for taking a chance by dedicating a spot in their series for this work.

Without my family I could not be where I am. My mom and dad worked hard to make sure I had everything possible to succeed. Without their help, I would not have made it to college, let alone going to graduate school and completing my doctorate.

My beautiful wife and daughter gave me continuous encouragement and love that drove me even on the hardest days.

Thank you to Lizzie and Daniel for reading this book more times than they cared to.

As always, any mistakes found in the text are my own.

Introduction

Why a Religion of White Supremacy?

In 1941, in the industrial center of the Midwest, Warner Sallman painted the most iconic image of American Christian iconography. While this was not Sallman's first attempt at creating the picture, what Sallman painted is the best-selling piece of art in U.S. history. Sallman's *Head of Christ* (1941) forever changed the image of the Christian savior. Sallman's Christ had long flowing brown hair, a brown hair beard, a defined yet gentle face, and a long white robe that draped his shoulders and upper chest, and he was bathed in the heavenly glow of an illuminating whiteness and light. In this image, Sallman depicted a strong and compassionate savior. The popularity of Sallman's *Head of Christ* is undeniable in the second half of the American century. *Head of Christ* was reproduced at least 500 million times by the early 1990s. In all, Warner Sallman sold one billion reproductions of his religious art, but none of his other pieces ever compared to *Head of Christ* as a cultural icon of the twentieth century.[1] *Head of Christ* became the image to depict religiosity in the post–World War II American culture, with the image being reproduced in any manner in which it could be sold. Even Billy Graham used Sallman's *Head of Christ* in his revivals as he crisscrossed the country saving souls.[2] The image of Christ depicted in Sallman's painting became much more than a painting in the United States, as some even described it as a photograph.[3]

Sallman's *Head of Christ* points to a peculiar reality within the societal structure of the United States. His work became a cultural icon of religiosity in the United States and was elevated to a mythological level. In this way, *Head of Christ* is a symptomatic representation of the American experience. It has been sold in numbers unlike any other cultural item in the American society and has forever changed the image of Christ in the country.[4] The social imagination of the United States envisions Jesus now as a white male with long, flowing brown hair and in a white robe. The indelible image of

Jesus presented in Sallman's *Head of Christ* led to the argument presented in these pages. *Head of Christ* is not the cause of what follows, but is the result of a rarely comprehended cognitive conditioning of the American psyche.

The American experience is one of white supremacy. So I am not misunderstood, *the American experience is one of white supremacy.* American life from the colonial age to the Age of Obama is and has always been determined by a white supremacist society that functions through the symbols of Christian symbolism and white power. As James H. Cone and Cornel West, among other scholars, have argued, the history of the United States is littered and plagued by the murder, oppression, and subjugation of nonwhites for the benefits of white society, and oftentimes has been ordained by American Christian myths and institutions shaped during the modern epoch. In what follows, I weave together the various fabrics of American history through an approach I call theo-historical in order to demonstrate how white supremacist Christianity was constructed and operated and how it continues to maintain American society for whites and for the betterment of whites.

To begin with, it is important to clarify some very important points so as to ensure there is no confusion of the argument that is to come in the following pages. First, this is not a work seeking to demonize whites or those who perceive themselves as white in the United States; rather, I am seeking to honestly assess the realms of U.S. history in terms of race-based oppression and the theological (Christian) myths and symbols that justified, maintained, and promoted a society based on white supremacy with all its spoken and unspoken benefits for the heirs of this legacy. Second, this work should be understood as a critique of the religion of white supremacy. There are points in the pages to come that could read as my support for the religion of white supremacy. This is simply *not* the case. My intention at points is to create a theoretical construction of the rationale of the religion of white supremacy. Third, many who read this book will wonder if in using the term "theo-historical," I am envisioning a different term for historical theology. The simple answer to this question is no. The task which I take historical theology to be is the study of theological developments and trajectories that were constructed in particular contexts.[5] The study of the historical situation of theology is important, but not the primary method undertaken in this project. I am using a theo-historical method in order to focus this work on the use of theology, not in the maintenance of the Christian faith, dogma and/ or doctrine, but rather, in the historical development of the modern project of capitalism and colonialism as witnessed in the genocide of Amerindians and the use of chattel slavery in the United States to drastically enhance the psychological, material, and capital wealth of white people. The reason for combining theology and history into one term is to reference the sacred symbolism of Christian theology in the construction of white supremacist

Christianity as it manifests in the United States. This theological history baptizes whiteness as the sacred color pigment of the Holy as envisioned in the blessedness of white flesh.

In analyzing the intersection of the theological and historical, I bring together two different approaches to the religiosity of white supremacy. The most direct connection would be to Willie James Jennings's *The Christian Imagination: Theology and the Origins of Race.* Jennings' acuity demonstrates the intimate relationship between the genesis of modernity, Christian theology, and the perpetuation of a corrupt social imagination.[6] He establishes how theology and modernity are inseparable in the operations of race. *The Christian Imagination* shows how the formation of this nexus manifests in the early stage of colonialism. In his approach, Jennings demonstrates, through the analysis of history, the antecedents of racism and what would become white supremacy. His work in history shows the importance of understanding the past in interpreting the present theological situation, but *The Christian Imagination* does not fully take this step to codify the effect of history on the present situation.

The second approach is James W. Perkinson's theological deconstruction of whiteness in *White Theology: Outing Supremacy in Modernity.* In this work, Perkinson focuses on the contemporary manifestations of white supremacy and how even its apparent secular nature is inherently theological.[7] In using a theological lens to culturally analyze society, Perkinson demonstrates how to read societal shifts and upheavals by unpacking the theologicalness of life. In this way, the action of white supremacy, either by persons or by institutions, becomes understood as a religious act. Unlike Jennings, who sought to construct the theological predecessors to modern racism, Perkinson is using theology to show how white supremacy dictates the operative mechanisms of the world.

Both Jennings and Perkinson provide models through which further exploration of the theologicalness of white supremacy can be revealed in modern society, but neither fully seeks to connect the historical and the theological in their argument. Jennings focuses primarily on the theological developments of racism centuries ago, much in the same way intellectual history seeks to interpret the progression of different thoughts and ideas. On the other hand, Perkinson's work reads more from the standpoint of Black Theology or Critical Race Theory. The framework of the theo-historical incorporates Jennings and Perkinson's approaches. It is not primarily history or theology. What I am constructing through the idea of theo-historical is an argument grounded within both disciplines. The theo-historical seeks to construct theology through the analysis of the past. As such, theology is tempered by historical evidence, in order to avoid the pitfalls of the *ahistorical* theologies that created the mechanisms of racism and white supremacy.

THEO-HISTORICAL METHODOLOGY

I understand the theo-historical method as a way to interpret lived theologies.[8] While the discipline of theology, particularly those engaged in the Protestant Christian tradition, primarily focuses on the dogmas and doctrines of the faith, lived theology is an investigation of how people envision and operate within a religio-cultural system. To fully comprehend these ways of being necessitates engagement in both history and theology. The ways in which people comprehend their place in the world are intimately connected to the past, particularly on the issues of race and racism. In this way, this project is working through the dualism of reading history through a theological lens, while at the same time, interpreting the theological in contemporary society filtered through historical precedence. This duality enables a more complete picture of the intersection of Christianity and white supremacy because of its equal commitments.

Before moving ahead with the body of my argument it is necessary to establish the foundations of the work. In doing this, the reader will understand what I am and am not attempting in this project. First, this work is designed to be a conversation between history and theology. For this reason, the work will move between both disciplines by bringing them together in ways that are not traditionally conducted. This could cause the book to have a sense of identity crisis, but the intention is to show how connected the idea of white supremacy is to both American forms of Protestant theology and the history of race in the United States. This working together makes this project possible. I do not see myself as a historian who tries to employ theology (by which I mean the discipline of theology) to extrapolate on the arguments made in the past. Yet, I also do not see my work as a product of theology. I am not constructing or deconstructing the dogmas and doctrines of theology as someone who is concerned with justifying or maintaining a faith system, that is, Protestant Christianity. While it is true in a formal sense that I am culturally and socially connected to a branch of the Protestant Christian tradition, this does not mean my work is primarily concerned with affirming white Protestant Christianity. As a scholar of religion, I seek to present an honest account of the intersections between white supremacy and white Protestantism whether or not my own religious tradition is implicated in the religion of white supremacy.

In this way, my work aligns with Mark Lewis Taylor's idea of the theological. In *The Theological and the Political*, Taylor proposes a new way of understanding theology (not the discipline of theology) as "a discourse that discerns and critically reflects upon the motions of power . . . "[9] by which I see the ideas of theology as a way of reading history and current cultural and societal conditions. This enables me to construct a system in which historical events can be read as symbols within a line of tradition that makes sense of how and why the United States operates the way it does economically, politically, and religiously. As such, I can use the sources and meanings of theology as a discipline to inform my work without "sanctioning its traditional concerns as a guild discipline."[10] This concept will seem odd to an academic within the guild of theology and even to those outside of these conversations, but I want to make it clear that this work is designed to critically deconstruct how theology (as it pertains to doctrine) mutated with the political within U.S. culture to construct a system of knowing in the contemporary that builds on William R. Jones's concept of "divine racism." This might sound confusing, but in essence, I seek to comprehend how our societal systems are constructed today in *areligious* sorts of ways, yet are first molded and shaped in very cosmological ways by Protestant Christians. For this reason, it is necessary to move beyond the idea of white supremacy (as it functions in a seemingly *areligious* manner) to a paradigm that calls the institutionalized structures of whiteness for what they are: a religion. Even more pointedly, white supremacy is not a system of ultimate concern that is constructed in an *ex nihilio* fashion in the United States. The very bedrock of white supremacy is constructed out of the symbols and traditions of Protestant Christianity as they developed over the past five centuries.

The deliberate framing of this work as theological rather than as theology enables the implementation of the theo-historical by stripping away the rigidity of theology's guild talk for a culturally driven reading of the mechanisms that could create a religious system. Unlike theology, the use of the theo-historical method places all sources on equal footing. This means I do not consider one theological source to be more important or above all others. This means that while many Christian theologians place sacred scriptures as the first source, my work considers scripture to be on the same footing as experience, history, and tradition. In this way, Anthony Pinn's humanistic theology becomes a way to construct and interpret the cultural and historical as sources for a theological system. Much like Pinn's humanistic theology, the only real way for the theo-historical to work is through the equal reading of sources in order to pinpoint the religious in the mundane, and then to be able to analyze the religious in historically grounded ways with an eye to the future. Inherent in the theo-historical is the tension of being a historian and theologian in a single breath.

If done correctly, the semiotics of the historical and theological become clear. The theological is the way in which the world is viewed as a religious organism. This does not mean, with the Christian tradition in mind, that every act taken in the world is manifested in and through God or the Christ. I am pointing to how every act has meaning. The theological provides a form from which these meanings are interpreted in order to ascertain which meanings hold ultimacy over cultural systems and those who operate within them. As a historian, I search primary documents to understand the motivations of the subjects of the American white supremacist system. This means seeking to comprehend the writings, speeches, and newspapers of the time. This work is done in association with the background issues that influenced the beliefs that were determinative in history.

In returning to Pinn's work, his analysis of Starbucks in *The End of God-Talk* is illustrative of how I envision the theological as cultural analysis. In deconstructing the importance of Starbucks, Pinn demonstrates how the coffee chain is not simply a place for coffee drinkers, but rather can become a place of meaning or human connection.[11] Pinn's ability to establish that Starbucks transitioned from a place of overpriced coffee to something much more for its adherents establishes a form of cultural production as more than just space. Starbucks's ability to offer itself as a place of "complex subjectivity" means that—to those who participate—its status within their lives is much greater than any outsider might be able to understand. Pinn's focus on "complex subjectivity" enables the theological in a variety of ways that are unhinged from more traditional constructs of religious expressions, to see how the Holy can be more than a divine expression.

The theological sees all cultural expression as a possible site of religious expression. Without a doubt, this viewpoint can become too broad to be a meaningful adjudicator of religious analysis, and yet, more precise methods are susceptible to missing discrete yet powerful cultural forces, for example white supremacy, as holding religious character. It is precisely this broad view of ultimacy that provides the necessary creativity that reveals the full extent in which ultimacy is found in white supremacy in the United States. The concept of ultimacy is integral to the formation of this work. Ultimacy is directly derived from Paul Tillich's argument that whatever is a person's ultimate concern is god for them.[12] To this extent, I also see the idea of ultimate concern as constructing a religious system. This means that for the sake of this book, the power of whiteness becomes the ultimate concern of the American nation. This is possible due to the initial formation of the nation on the premise of the dichotomy of Christian and heathen that morphs into different forms for different eras to meet the needs of political power. As such, this dichotomy acts as a universal belief of superiority of Christian over and against heathens of the early seventeenth century. This distinction would later change to meet the construction of racial concepts, the turn to secular language by society during the Enlightenment and after, and the contemporary need for coded racial language in politics. What remains, though, is the universality of the superiority of Christianity that would turn to white supremacy by the founding of the United States a hundred and fifty years after the Puritan use of heathenism.

This argument is possible because Tillich understood that theological ideas must have experiential basis. "Universals can become matters of ultimate concern only through their power of representing concrete experiences."[13] The history presented in these pages proves the universality of white supremacy as an ultimate concern. The moments laid out demonstrate the ultimate concern of the United States as the perpetuation of a system that empowers whites while ensuring the subservience of other people. I will expound on the concept of ultimacy further in the introduction.

The second piece of the theo-historical method takes the hypothesis created by the theological and tests it against the realities of history. The reason for this second aspect of the method is to ensure that the application of the theological is more than a mere theory. This is a major source of weakness for theology. The construction of theology does not necessarily need a control mechanism, as history does. This becomes problematic because in the Christian tradition the control mechanism becomes the primacy of sacred scriptures. The establishment of sacred scriptures as the base for these theological systems is not inherently dangerous, but at the same time, history tells a different story. The use of Christian scripture to justify innumerable unspeakable acts begs whether its use as a control is fully beneficial. For this reason, the theo-historical relies on history to test theological systems. Throughout this work, the theo-historical paradigm uses cultural analysis to construct a theological system that proves the religious nature of white supremacy. For this argument to work, a second step must be taken to temper this theory with history as its control mechanism. Through this second step, the theological claims of white supremacy as religion are proven by history.

While this work focuses on the formation of white supremacy as a religion, the theo-historical method can be used to investigate any possible forms of religious expression.

WHY A RELIGION OF WHITE SUPREMACY?

What do I mean by the religion of white supremacy? First and foremost, I do *not* mean tattooed, bald, neo-Nazis, nor do I mean men in white robes burning crosses. This must be made clear because I do not want a reader with white skin to think I am simply writing about extremists. I am writing about whites and whiteness as a whole. This particularly includes me as a white Protestant, heterosexual, and male with the means to live comfortably in twenty-first-century America. This means I am writing as much about myself as I am writing as an academic observer of the particularities of society in the United States. So, what does white supremacist Christianity mean? According to the *Merriam-Webster Dictionary*, "white supremacy" is "a doctrine based on a belief that the white race is inherently superior to other races and that white people should have control over people of other races." This definition is particularly important because it points to more than just a simple belief in the supremacy of white people, but rather, an ontic foundation of the supremacy of white people, and through this ontological doctrine, the inherent right to assert this supremacy over others for the benefit of the white race. But of course, simply using the dictionary to define "white supremacy" does not fully demonstrate the meaning of white supremacist Christianity and the loaded imagery that such a term can and will transmit.

In focusing on the religion of white supremacy as a category of investigation in this work, there is an inseparable quality between the establishment of and the continuation of white supremacy and the religiosity known as Christianity. Many purveyors of the Christian faith in the United States point to the foundation of this country as a Christian nation—the belief of the United States as God's chosen nation—and the need to secure Christianity in the future fabric of the nation. These arguments are important to what I am intimating is an inseparable nature connecting Christianity and the doctrine of the supremacy of white people. In 2008, The Pew Forum on Religion and Public Life published the *U.S. Religious Landscape Survey*, in which 35,000 people were surveyed, and of that number, 78.4% of respondents declared themselves as Christian. In addition to this, 51.3% self-classified themselves as some form of Protestant, while 23.9% identify as Roman Catholic.[14] Whether the people surveyed are regular practicing Protestant Christians or not, one can rightly assume that over three-quarters of the United States identify as Christian with over half the population with some sort of Protestant affiliation. This information is key in understanding how normative the Christian religion is within the United States and how a Christian moral code and ethos necessarily permeates or drives the cultural and social contract of the nation.

The connection of white supremacy and Christianity points to a way of interpreting U.S. history that makes available a theoretical framework for analyzing the historical realities through a theological reading. In this way, the bringing together of white supremacy and Christianity becomes a method in which the symbolism of white supremacy is deciphered in order to unmask the moral/social structures of white society and their unbreakable bonds with the Christian faith. To this end, the mundane operations of American society are designed and controlled in order to maintain the superiority of whiteness through the moral and symbolic codes of the Christian faith. The theo-historical method of analysis provides the lens through which the demonic nature of white supremacy is revealed through the analysis of history. Reading U.S. history in this particular fashion enables the creative/destructive nature of white supremacy to be unpacked, which demonstrates how this religious system is maintained through the elevation of whiteness beyond a scientific or political measure to a divine status. Put another way, the white supremacist faith system gives ultimate meaning to those who embody the particularities of the demonic divine as symbolically manifested in the white Christ.

Returning to Pinn's humanistic theology proves instructive in demonstrating the relevance of white supremacy as a religious idea through the idea of p(l)ace. In developing p(l)ace as an intentional locale for intentional meaning, Pinn says that the ordinary can offer more than a religious idea.[15] I see his idea of p(l)ace as applicable to the formation of the United States. As this project shows, the United States became an intentional locale for specific people and, in that, also offered an intentional meaning. The British colonies, and later the United States, constructed this specific geographic area as a place for whites to come and gather together in their commonness.

To be sure, there were many differences between the whites who came to North America, and yet, a common meaning was found in their differences from the indigenous cultures and the peoples from Africa. The importance here is found in the common feeling of superiority among the people who would become a part of the American nation. Like Pinn's understanding of Starbucks, the United States is a place that offers a radically different perspective depending on whether one is seen as a member of the nation or not. The sacredness is found in the being and knowing of the ruling body. No matter how hard a member of the out-groups tried, they could never understand the true ultimacy found in the power of what would become known as white. The concept of p(l)ace applies only to those who reside within the United States with the particularities of whiteness; otherwise, the power of ultimacy could not be fully understood as a benefit. It is the specialness of whiteness with the specific locale of the United States that led to the creation of meaning. It is only through these elements that a religion of white supremacy could really become a reality in this geographical space. Seeing the United States as p(l)ace for whites makes intelligible the historical events used in this work to prove the theologicalness of white supremacy.

P(l)ace brings together white supremacy and Christianity into the demonic form of white supremacist Christianity. Tillich's discussion of the existence of the demonic shows how the demonic operates, and it has similarities to earlier understandings of sin. Tillich argues that the demonic operates on the level of the soul, but this should not be understood as the demon spirits of Christian myths or for that matter any other religious myth; rather, it is more like the personality level within a human. In this way, Tillich is setting up the demonic as something that is not contained in the body, but rather in the parts of the human that determine actions and emotions, similar to how Augustine understands the will. This means that the demonic is more effective in persons in whom the power of freedom and self-mastery prevail, particularly as the personality starts to control a person in such a way that allows something else to take control of its personality that results in spirit distorting. "The demonic is visible only when the cleavage of the ego has an ecstatic character, so that with all its destructiveness it is still creative."[16]

The United States was the place in which Christianity and white supremacy could come together to form a new religious construct that makes white supremacy and the Christian tradition inseparable. The historical cases in chapters three through five prove the unique quality of the United States as the p(l)ace of white supremacist Christianity. This means that the locale of the United States created a special meaning within the minds of those who adhere to white supremacist Christianity such that in one moment the nation can be described as a Christian nation and also be a place of unequal power possessed by a particular racial group from the historical inception to the contemporary present.

While the historical examples presented in this work point to particularly egregious moments in U.S. history, there are also instances that break this mold. The work of John Brown and other abolitionists fighting to end slavery, the involvement of white clergy in the Civil Rights Movement, and the coalition of white supporters who helped elect President Barack Obama are points in history where the foundations of white supremacist Christianity are momentarily chipped away to reveal a possibly new paradigm. This work does not seek to diminish the work of those who have fought for racial justice, but it instead points to an overarching trajectory within the day-to-day operations of white supremacist Christianity. Each of these examples can be lifted up as moments of hope in U.S. history, and yet, one must also remember that each of these moments had unintended consequences. The work of abolitionists gave way to the rise of Jim/Jane Crow. The Civil Rights Movement led to a coalition of predominately white persons seeking to overturn these new laws. Finally, the election of Barack Obama resulted in the escalation of explicit white supremacy returning to mainstream politics in the election of Donald Trump.

There are other historical moments that complicate the history of white supremacist Christianity, but the goal here is to demonstrate how particular moments in U.S. history have brought together the Christian tradition and beliefs in white superiority. Instances of resistance should be viewed as the exceptions that they are. This does not mean that they do not give hope of a different future. It does mean that this cannot be the dominant narrative. Many in the Christian tradition point to Dietrich Bonhoeffer as the model of Christian resistance to Nazism and the murder of millions of Jews and others.[17] What these stories of Bonhoeffer's resistance fail to tell is the sad truth of the Christian faith in Nazi Germany. For the most part, the Christian churches adopted the Nazification of their beliefs.[18] The legacy of the German

Christians is all but forgotten among contemporary American Christians, yet the Nazi Party would not have been able to maintain its power without this support.[19] The point is that the actions of abolitionists and others would not be necessary without a larger history of complicity, and this history is what needs to be understood in order to comprehend the matrices of power that dominate society.

Although the primary lens of this project is the theological nature of white supremacist Christianity and how it is shaped through history, it is also important to note the political realities of maintaining this system. Without the use of politics to create the dynamics necessary to maintain the dominance of whiteness, the *polis*, as shaped by the particularities of the white Christ, would not be possible. With this in mind, Charles Mills's *The Racial Contract* provides incredible insight into the political ways in which a social contract of white supremacy has developed in modernity. Mills strongly states the case for an understanding of white supremacy as a political system in such a way that makes it clear how racism permeates all levels of Western society that it can cause the collapse of formal systems for the sole purpose of maintaining the primary political system that benefits only those who meet the pigmentation qualification. In this project, I take Mills's argument in a separate, yet intimately connected, direction. I argue that white supremacy is more than a political system; it is first and foremost a religious system. What do I mean by a religious system? First of all, I am not speaking of a micro-religious concept, like Christian groups that meet for an hour on Sunday; rather, my argument has its foundation on the macro level. I am seeking to expand the idea of religion beyond its particularities, and focus on the commonalties of religious systems.

When interpreting religious expression on a macro level, the threads that weave together white supremacy and Christianity become discernable. This is achieved by looking at the common denominators that drive American society. Tillich's theological analysis of ultimacy is helpful in understanding how macro-level religious experience works.

Man, like every living being, is concerned about many things, above all about those which condition his very existence, such as food and shelter. But man, in contrast to other living being, has spiritual concerns—cognitive, aesthetic, social, political. Some of them are urgent, often extremely urgent, and each of them as well as the vital concerns can claim ultimacy for a human life or the life of a social group. If it claims ultimacy it demands the total surrender of him who accepts this claim, and it promises total fulfillment even if all other claims have to be subjected to it or rejected in its name. If a national group makes the life and growth of the nation its ultimate concern, it demands that all other concern, economic well-being, health and life, family, aesthetic and cognitive truth, justice and humanity, be sacrificed.[20]

Tillich's understanding of ultimate concern is strongly based on his experience with the rise of National Socialism and the construction of Nazi Germany, in which the nation's ontic state was more important than the ontological self. While it may be argued that this system of nation as religion exists in many different ways, past and future, this is not my concern within this project. I believe that within the United States a more powerful ultimate concern operates within the body politic that functions as a macro-level religious system: white supremacy.

It may seem odd to some to posit white supremacy as a religious system, but it has an ontological social quality that has created and continues to create a body politic centered on the preservation of the white race and privilege. As such, the body politic's ultimate concern is the preservation of white supremacy. While the body's assertion of white supremacy has changed in the 400 years since the arrival of British colonizers in the North America, the foundational concern of the colony, and later the nation, was the preservation of white superiority. As this project proceeds, a theo-historical account of racism will be constructed that demonstrates the intimate connection between the status of whiteness and one's place within the American psyche that does more than simply connect people of similar hues. This religious racialism justifies the active and passive destruction of the Other within the larger society, whether the persons be African-American, indigenous, or even visually perceived as white.

Tillich's use of time and space are established as categories within his system to understand the correlation of being and finitude.[21] The interplay of time and space cognitively makes real the idea that for something to live, it must also reach death. For this reason, time is an indispensable category of life because of the unshakable truth that to be born immediately starts the process toward death. Time is a constant and must always move forward. Time cannot move backward or remain motionless.[22] The weight of time leads to a power struggle within the mind of people and groups.

The reality of time is that it cannot stand alone. While time is defined by its ever-present move into the future regardless of the desire of humans to cheat death, space provides humans a place to understand their being.[23] In space, people find meaning in spite of the continuous move to the final reality of finitude. Space can act as a barrier to the realities of time. In this way, space can enable a place for persons to overcome the realities of time. To find space means to fulfill the "ontological necessity" of achieving the material reality of taking form in a body, but it also means that one attaches to a particular place that becomes one's own in the way that one claims a home or country.[24] While this understanding of space demonstrates the physical necessities of space, it also has a social element that enables people to connect beyond themselves through membership in a social network, like a group that operates through a particular "structure of values and meanings."[25] White supremacist Christianity manifests and maintains itself through the construction of social space much in the same way that people find identity through connection to a religious tradition or even a professional sports franchise.

Tillich points to the power of space in providing meaning to humans in light of the constant weight of finitude by showing how a group can find purpose through the construction of an identity, particularly in the drive of nationalism. The purpose of nationalism is not the same as the pride one takes in being a member of a particular nation, as Independence Day can call forth patriotic emotions in even the most cynical members of a society. Nationalism takes on the dynamic of ultimacy. The formation of nationalism transforms the meaning-making identity of one's national space that operates alongside other spaces in the form of nations and creates a form of creative destruction. The elevation of national pride from a place of meaning to one of ultimacy naturally instills an "us against them" mentality that is what Tillich defines as paganism.[26] In this way, nationalism becomes about "the adoration of earth and soil, not of soil generally but of this special soil, and not of earth generally but of the divine powers connected with this special section of the earth."[27] The combination of national identity and the ultimate is seen in the construction of Nazism in interwar Germany and the preservation of imperial Rome. The ultimacy of social space is most easily discernable in the guise of nationalism, yet it is not the only manifestation of sacred space.

Sacred space is found in many different forms. Tillich's understanding of the symbolism of the Kingdom of God represents the unity of time and space.[28] By applying time and space to the Kingdom of God as a symbol, Tillich is showing that his idea of space is not limited to its physical connection of meaning to an object as discernable as the geographical boundaries of a nation. The symbol of the Kingdom of God points to the possibility that less discernable elements can be elevated to the status of ultimacy. White supremacist Christianity acts in such a manner. The religion of whiteness takes the commonality of pigmentation and a system of thought and meaning that binds a particular group of people and elevates it to the basis of ultimacy. The inseparable mixture of white flesh with the systems of the Christian faith creates a power of being in which it is inconceivable for one to deprive himself or herself of this sacred space.[29]

Tillich argues that space in its proper form operates as a "beside-each-otherness" in the way that groups of people may find meaning in a nation while at the same time recognizing that other nations coexist in this system.[30] When space provides meaning in spite of finitude, the operative quality enables the creation of other spaces of meaning. Elevating a space to the realm of ultimacy necessarily destroys "beside-each-otherness" and replaces it with "against-each-otherness."[31] Elevating a particular space to the place of ultimacy means that no other spaces may stand alongside in the place of ultimacy. To do so would delegitimize the ultimacy of one's own space and would directly result in the destruction of ultimacy. The elevation of space beyond the limits of finitude necessarily means no other space can stand beside it. The making of space into a sacred space raises the meaning of space to a "spatial god."[32] To find meaning through a spatial god means taking the creative elements that enable space to create meaning and shifting this creativity to the destruction of other forms of spatial meaning. To permit "beside-each-otherness" is antithetical to the idea of sacred space. To make a space sacred, as in the spatiality of white supremacist Christianity, necessitates the elimination of all other space. Conceiving white supremacist Christianity as sacred space constructs the conditions by which theology adds to the conceptual framework of whiteness.

WHY NOW?

The 2008 election of Barack Obama as the first African-American president of the United States seemed to many to be the culmination of the American belief in "the land of free and the home of the brave." Soon after the election, people, particularly in the media, used the election of President Barack Obama as evidence that the United States had rejected its racial past and that the United States was now a society where anyone, from any race, could succeed and fulfill their own "American Dream." People flooded Washington, D.C., on January 20, 2009, to witness the United States coming full circle from its history of slavery (in which the city of Washington, D.C., and the White House were built on the backs of black bodies) to swear in a black president.

It did not take long after the inauguration of President Obama for the narrative of a postracial United States to become muddled with a different narrative. This version argued that there was a great conspiracy to elect President Obama and that he was actually a Muslim radical born in Kenya who had usurped the U.S. Constitution and would destroy the country. This movement that was informally known as "birthers" was combined with another group who saw the election of President Obama as a socialist takeover of the country, evidenced by the passage of the hotly contested Affordable Care Act. Many in the United States, including the media, see the birther movement now as a fringe radical group, but in the first years of the Obama administration, 47% of U.S. citizens either thought President Obama illegally became president or did not know where he was born.[33]

Political commentators see these two movements as an example of the extreme polarization of the United States, where the population is seemingly split between two political parties, but there is another explanation that the media and others have ignored because it calls into question the myth of a postracial United States. The reality is that since President Barack Hussein Obama's election on November 4, 2008, there has been an underlying narrative of white supremacy permeating politics. Movements like "birtherism" and the Tea Party sought to discredit the Obama administration with seemingly legitimate political differences. While some might simply disagree with Obama's political views, there is another element that is prevalent in these protests and disagreements. This can be found in the 2012 Republican Party nominee for president. On August 24, 2012, Mitt Romney remarked, "No one's ever asked to see my birth certificate. They know that this is the place that I was born and raised."[34] This poignant comment on the eve of the Republican National Convention demonstrated the uneasiness of the racial undertones facing the country in light of President Obama's election.

Why would people question the citizenship of one political candidate and not another? Is there something about Mitt Romney that is quintessentially more American than President Obama? Is it possible that the United States is not as postracial or colorblind as the society would like to believe in the aftermath of the 2008 presidential election? These questions come to the essential nature of this project. In this book, I offer a conceptual history of the United States that takes seriously the role of theology and the church in establishing racial categories and the myth of white supremacy, which has permeated the history of this country from its earliest settlers in the seventeenth century through the present situation, where the citizenship of the president of the United States of America can be contested. By doing this, I show the importance of Christian theology and the Christian church, particularly Protestantism, in the formation of racial hierarchies that have informed the creation of the American experience as a particular form of whiteness.[35]

Analyzing the election of President Obama demonstrates the different levels in which whiteness operates. The majority of white people experience what Charles Mills calls an "epistemology of ignorance" that enables them to construct a societal myth that ignores the realities of societal conditions through a narrative that justifies their position.[36] This blindness operates in most whites on passive levels, and this is one reason President Obama won the election. This all changed after the election when active voices of whiteness became prominent in media conversations. Groups, like birthers or the Tea Party Movement, focused on ways that President Obama was threatening American democracy, either by his unlawful ascension to the presidency or by his alleged socialist policies that were going to result in wealth redistribution[37], death panels[38], and ultimately tyrannical communism.[39] The media gave significant attention to persons like Glenn Beck and Rush Limbaugh, who stoked these fears, but rarely did the media make the connection to the overwhelmingly white composition of these groups. One explanation for why this happened is that persons who operate with active whiteness, those who engage in white supremacy, were able to construct a narrative of President Obama that enabled more whites to see the president as a threat.

The culmination of the repudiation of President Obama is evidenced in the election of Donald Trump as Obama's successor. Trump campaigned on the racial animus developed by the Tea Party Movement and his own reputation as anti-Obama. Trump's ability to seize on the sentiments of many whites that Obama was not a citizen of the United States enabled him to become the standard bearer of a particular brand of "truth" held by many whites in the United States.

Trump's use of immigrant stereotypes, Islamophobia, and coded racial language made him the ideal candidate to restore the prominence of white supremacy in the United States. The rise of hate crimes against blacks, immigrants, Jews, and Muslims shows that Trump's followers are emboldened by his election and the rhetoric of America first.[40] And yet, the political campaign tells the story a particular sort of America: One where whites are the true standard bearer of the term American.

This context proves the necessity of this project for the present moment. Some prognostication sees the time of white supremacy in the U.S. culture as waning. I do not agree with this assessment. White supremacy is too strong of a cultural force in the United States and its history to fade away. The lesson history provides in this moment is that the United States will never be free of its founding religious dogma of white superiority. The truth is, while some see a colorblind society, our racist past will always be bubbling just below the surface and just needs the right confluence of events to explode once again. This lesson can be seen in the interwar period in Germany. Nazi ideology was not created in the vacuum of post–World War I political turmoil. Centuries of cultural conditioning made possible the rise of Nazism and its race-based ideology.

So too, the lesson should be the same in the United States. This argument is more complex than "history repeats itself." The religion of white supremacy is at the core of the United States. The events discussed in later chapters bear the fruit of this line of thinking. What is seen in the various historical moments is the way in which the content and focus of white supremacy may ebb and flow from the earliest British colonists to how contemporary Americans view the cultural landscape. What is constant is the belief in white supremacy. The ultimacy of white supremacy has held fast from the oxymoronic notion of "all men are created equal" being written by a slaveholder to the limitation of voting rights to ensure freedom. The ever-constant place of white supremacy in the United States is not an artifact of the past; rather, it is a living system in itself that seeks to maintain itself through its congregants.

The creation of the United States as a p(l)ace of white supremacy is a much more accurate insight to the present situation than arguments that claim its final breaths. To put it simply, the United States is a by-product of white supremacy; therefore, without white supremacy as its originator, the United States could not exist in its present manifestation. The United States as a by-product of white supremacy is evident in the response to President Obama's two terms in office. History will remember the election of the first African-American president, but will surely forget the vitriol of the moment. Most likely, future generations will remember the election of Obama and at the same time will not remember the rise of the birther movement and the Tea Party, nor that Donald Trump was elected in large part due to his use of racial animus to unite white voters. In essence, to forget is the privilege of whiteness. This book is intended to help whites not forget the power that white supremacy holds in the present moment. The history of the United States shown in these pages is a direct contradiction to the myth of colorblindness and show the importance of not forgetting the place of the past in shaping the future.

To say white supremacy is dead or dying in the United States only fifty years after Jim/Jane Crow does not take seriously the three and a half centuries in which white supremacy was the most visible aspect of the nation. When I set out to write this book, it was in response to the notion that the weight of white supremacy was shedding from the fabric of the nation. This is precisely the danger in this moment in history. People like myself enjoy the freedom of history's results to see the present as a new golden era of tranquility, yet those on the wrong side of U.S. history see little or no change. The siren song of whiteness blinds white eyes into seeing a society without race. This is exactly what the religion of white supremacy desires for those mesmerized by the song. In truth, the white supremacy of today has little difference from its past manifestations. While not as blatantly vicious in its attacks against nonwhites, the outcomes have changed very little over the course of history.

In light of this previous line of thinking, how does one start to read the legacy of white supremacy as a religious construct that is central to American society? First, it must be said that what follows throughout this project is indebted to three works that took the necessary steps to make this project possible. J Kameron Carter's *Race: A Theological Account* demonstrated the necessity for theology (as an academic discipline) to see race as a relevant category of theological exploration. Willie James Jennings's *The Christian Imagination: Theology and the Origins of Race* placed the modern idea of race within its historical context to prove its origins as a particular reading of the Christian tradition. Lastly, Christopher M. Driscoll's *White Lies: Race and Uncertainty in the Twilight of American Religion* took the necessary step of moving from discussions of race to the culprit of the system: white supremacy. Each of these works in their own way influenced the construction of *The Religion of White Supremacy in the United States*. While there is some difference of conclusion, this work would not be able to make the leap that it does without this previous research.

While the books previously mentioned precede this work, there are two books that are of particular importance to arguing for the idea of white supremacist Christianity. The first is James H. Cone's *The Cross and the Lynching Tree*. When I read this work, the idea of white supremacy haunting the United States took center stage in my thinking. Cone's biting critique of white society and white Christianity, in particular, led me down the rabbit hole of cultural and personal analysis. In his introduction, Cone stated, "If white Americans could look at the terror they inflicted on their own black population then they might be able to understand what is coming at them from others."[41] This quote led to this work less as a reality of academic research and more as a personal revelation of what Charles Mills calls a "signatory of the racial contract." While I "knew" the history of chattel slavery and the genocide of indigenous peoples, I did not know the reifying and ever-evolving history of white supremacy. The desire to know this history led me to the next book.

Edward J. Blum's *Reforging the White Republic: Race, Religion, and American Nationalism, 1865–1898* took the idea of seeing white supremacy as a problem within Christianity in the United States to its core feature. In unraveling the role of religion in the demise of Reconstruction, Blum led me to question if white supremacy was more than an aspect of the Christian imagination in the United States. While many people look to northern abolitionists as a model for breaking down the injustices of racism, few understand that it was the same people who drove the movement to reunite the North and South after the war.[42] The willingness of whites to forgo what Blum calls a "civic nationalism" for an "ethnic nationalism" points precisely to what I argue is the religion of white supremacy.[43] For these good Christian folk to abandon their civic religion for an ethnic one along the lines of white supremacist Christianity demonstrates the claim of ultimacy that is found in white supremacy. While many cultural observers would argue that people find ultimacy in a particular view of the American nation, even to the point where they will abandon their formal religious beliefs in a patriotic fervor, what Blum points to is a form of ultimacy that requires allegiance beyond the nation. The willingness of whites to destroy the racial promise after the Civil War in order to hold "fast to their vision of the United States as a nation ordained by God to be a 'white man's country'" shows that the nation might not be the center of religious expression in the United States.[44]

The rest of this book shows that the true religious core of the United States is the drive of white supremacy. This means that elements that many think are contributive factors to maintaining white supremacy in fact spring forth from the creative center. Concepts like the economy, nationalism, the polis, and war seem to act as constitutive elements that make up white supremacy, but the true cosmic power of white supremacy is that each of these parts are subject to the core. Whites have denied their best interests in each of these branches in order to reinforce the power of the white supremacist core.

The rest of the book will proceed in two parts. The first part is focused on the theological. The second part will apply the theological concepts from chapters 1 and 2 and analyze historical moments in the history of the United States. Chapter 1 will focus on the epistemology of whiteness and the ontology of white supremacy. This chapter begins by deconstructing the colonial idea of discovery and how the Europeans used it to establish their place as the rulers of the land "found" in North and South America. The idea of discovery becomes the starting point for understanding their European relationship with the people of the Americas. The belief in discovery provided the foundation for framing what Europeans saw as their unique characteristics through the lens of ultimacy. Understanding the world with a European center took the knowledge of superiority and made it more about who the Europeans were as people. Within the ontology of white supremacy, the knowledge of superiority led to the creation of a world in which the physical beingness of whiteness defined the superiority found in the brain.

Chapter 2 shifts from the epistemology of whiteness and the ontology of white supremacy to the how these ideas come together to form a soteriology of white flesh. The lens for this chapter is the image of Warner Sallman's *Head of Christ*. This chapter focuses on the transition from beliefs that make up white supremacy to a system that forms ultimacy as centered in white supremacy. This takes the necessary step from knowledge and embodiment to a centered act. The ultimacy of white supremacy transforms what would become understood as white in direct opposition to "heathenistic" people encountered in the Americas or forcibly brought to the Americas and those who would later seek refuge in the United States.

The theological foundation thus established, the second part turns to historical evidence to test the theological claims. These chapters will focus heavily on analyzing particular historical situations that reflect the theological pieces from chapters 1 and 2. Each chapter will begin and end with an explication of the relevant theological ideas and how they are applied in the historical moments.

Chapter 3 employs the epistemology of whiteness to the history of indigenous people in the United States. The chapter begins by recounting the use of divine violence against the Pequot people at Fort Mystic in the early seventeenth century. The history then turns to Jacksonian America and how the federal government framed the Five Civilized Nations to justify the Indian Removal Act of 1830. The removal of the civilized nations cosmologically established the white nation. The final section turns to how contemporary white supremacy uses the image of Indianness as a point of pride that points to a doubly complicated history through the representation of the Redskins as mascot for the National Football League team in Washington, D.C.

The fourth chapter shifts to how the ontology of white supremacy determined the relationship of whites with blacks in the century after the Civil War. This chapter analyzes the ontology of white supremacy reveals itself in the assault on black bodies. It begins by constructing the events of the Tulsa Race Riot in 1929. The chapter then looks at the lynching of two black men in Marion, Indiana. Finally, the chapter turns to social death experienced by blacks in northern industrial cities at the end of the Great Migration.

The fifth chapter turns to how whites have historically ensured the purity of the community. This chapter focuses on the power of law in establishing the parameters for who is and who is not white. The chapter begins by looking toward the Naturalization Act of 1790 that established that citizenship was only available to white persons. This law's passage by the First Congress of the United States proves the place of race consciousness from the outset of the United States. Next, the chapter shifts to the United States Supreme Court and how it used the idea of whiteness in the citizenship cases of Takao Ozawa and Bhagat Singh Thind in the 1920s. The chapter closes by showing how Arizona SB 1070 is a modern form of the Black Codes used in the American South after the Civil War. This shows how the antithesis of whiteness functions through the category of illegality.

The conclusion delves into the reality of the election of Donald Trump as Barack Obama's successor and how the theological history delineated throughout the book sees this historical moment as a logical result. The history of the religion of white supremacy made the election of Donald Trump more of an inevitability than most in the United States would want to believe. The conclusion moves from the reality of the Trump presidency to signaling future paths for better comprehending and elaborating the religion of white supremacy.

NOTES

1. David Morgan, "Sallman's *Head of Christ*: The History of an Image," *The Christian Century*, October 7, 1992.

2. Edward J. Blum and Paul Harvey, *The Color of Christ: The Son of God and the Saga of Race in America* (Chapel Hill: The University of North Carolina Press, 2011), 209.

3. Ibid.

4. Ibid., 12.

5. Alister E. McGrath, *Christian Theology: An Introduction*, 3rd ed. (New York: Blackwell Publishing, 2001), 144.

6. Willie James Jennings, *The Christian Imagination: Theology and the Origins of Race* (New Haven: Yale University Press, 2010), 6–7.

7. James W. Perkinson, *White Theology: Outing Supremacy in Modernity* (New York: Palgrave MacMillan, 2004), 2.

8. Ibid.

9. Mark Lewis Taylor, *The Theological and the Political: On the Weight of the World* (Minneapolis: Fortress Press, 2011), 9.

10. Ibid., 10.

11. Anthony B. Pinn, *The End of God-Talk: An African American Humanist Theology* (New York: Oxford University Press, 2012), 19.

12. Paul Tillich, *Systematic*, vol. 1, 211.

13. Ibid.

14. The Pew Forum of Religion and Public Life, *U.S. Religious Landscape Survey* (2008), accessed February 14, 2015, http://religions.pewforum.org/pdf/report-religious-landscape-study-full.pdf.

15. Pinn, *The End*, 16.

16. Paul Tillich, *The Interpretation of History*, ed. by Elsa L. Talmey (New York: Charles Scribner's Sons, 1936), 85–6.

17. Robert P. Ericksen, "Emerging From the Legacy? Protestant Churches and the 'Shoah,'" *Kirchliche Zeitgeschichte* 17, no. 2 (2004): 362.

18. Ibid., 375–6.

19. Ibid., 361.

20. Paul Tillich, *Dynamics of Faith* (New York: Perennial Classics, 2001), 1–2.

21. Tillich, *Systematic*, vol. 1, 192.

22. Tillich, *Theology of Culture*, 31.

23. Ibid.

24. Tillich, *Systematic*, vol. 1, 194.

25. Ibid.

26. Ibid.

27. Ibid., 32.

28. Tillich, *Systematic Theology*, vol. 3, 320.

29. Tillich, *Theology of Culture*, 33.

30. Ibid.

31. Ibid.

32. Ibid, 32.

33. "Poll: One in Four Americans Think Obama was not Born in U.S.," *CBS News*, April 21, 2011, Accessed on March 17, 2015.

34. "Romney Jokes about His Birth Certificate; Obama Campaign Accuses Him of Embracing Birtherism," *Washington Post*, August 24, 2012, accessed on February 13, 2015, http://www.washingtonpost.com/politics/romney-jokes-about-his-birth-certificate-obama-campaign-accuses-him-of-embracing-birtherism/2012/08/24/bda35810-ee14-11e1-b0eb-dac6b50187ad_story.html.

35. The idea of the American experience points to the presentation of myths and symbols that drive the United States as a people. This is largely shaped by the

mythological construction of U.S. history as seen in the History Channel's twelve-part documentary *America: The Story of Us* or the highly regulated dissemination of information in textbooks for American history and government classes during secondary education.

36. Mills, *The Racial*, 18.

37. "Who Pays for Obamacare," *Wall Street Journal*, July 12, 2010.

38. "Getting to the Source of the Death Panel Rumors," *New York Times*, August 14, 2009.

39. "Obama's Bright Smile Masks Socialist Push," *South Florida Sun-Sentinel*, September 13, 2009.

40. Mark Potok, "The Trump Effect," *Intelligence Report*, February 15, 2017, https://www.splcenter.org/fighting-hate/intelligence-report/2017/trump-effect.

41. Ibid., xix.

42. Edward J. Blum, *Reforging the White Republic: Race, Religion, and American Nationalism, 1865–1898* (Baton Rouge: Louisiana State University Press, 2007), 3.

43. Ibid.

44. Ibid., 48.

Part I

THE THEOLOGICAL FOUNDATIONS OF WHITE SUPREMACY

Chapter 1

The Religion of White Supremacy

A preliminary construction of a theology of whiteness through the concepts of epistemology and ontology will provide the foundation for the religion of whiteness by unveiling its drive for the ultimate. This chapter demonstrates how each category is necessary to the foundation of the theology of whiteness and shows how each concept builds on the previous. With the theological foundation laid in this chapter, the next chapter applies these concepts to show how the theology of whiteness operates from a demonic model. I begin the chapter by building how an epistemology of whiteness through the colonial mind-set of heathen as juxtaposed to Christianity, and how the right of domination, as justified based on religion, shifted to the correlation of white superiority and black inferiority by the turn of the nineteenth century. Here, epistemology is taken to mean the processes of knowledge consumption and creation. As such, the epistemology of whiteness signifies the ways in which whiteness is constructed and maintains itself through dissemination. The second piece of the chapter shows how the epistemology of whiteness then manifested into an ontology of white supremacy. The ontological construction of white supremacy did not appear simultaneously in relation to indigenous persons, blacks, or whites, yet the ontological separation of white and nonwhite followed a similar path to the white embodiment of superiority and ultimately the ontological assault against nonwhite bodies.

EPISTEMOLOGY OF WHITENESS

To frame the epistemology of whiteness, I begin not with history but rather with the contemporary realities of the American body politic. Many scholars and political pundits who discuss race/ism in the Obama era seek to frame their work either with Barack Obama's election-night speech or with Chief Justice John Robert's swearing in President Obama on January 20, 2009, but I think this does an injustice to the state of white hegemony even during the time of the first nonwhite male president. Due to their importance, I return to Mitt Romney's comments on August 24, 2012, where he spoke in front of 10,000 supporters in Commerce, Michigan, and said, "No one's ever asked to see my birth certificate. They know that this is the place where both of us were born and raised."[1] Mitt Romney's comments ten weeks before Election Day were curious for a candidate running for the highest elected office in the United States. It was no secret that his comments were in direct reference to a political movement that sought to disprove President Obama's right to hold the office of the presidency that received support from Donald Trump, among others.[2] What neither Romney nor the national media discussed was the similar family stories of Obama and Romney. Both men were born into families with American mothers and non-American fathers. Romney's father was born in Mexico and Obama's father in Kenya. Both Romney and Obama had parents who were not a part of the religious mainstream, with Romney's family being members of the Latter Day Saints and Obama's father being an observer of Islam while his mother was Christian. Clearly, both men did not follow the perceived path to the American presidency—so what makes Romney more reliably American than Obama? I posit the reason for Romney's acceptability within American society is his perceived connection to the psychological wages of whiteness.[3] Romney's whiteness and Obama's lack of whiteness, even though his mother was white, has a much longer history of admission in U.S. society than the advent of the "Birther" Movement in 2009. The Birthers' drive to nullify the presidency of Barack Obama can be connected to the very foundations of white society in the Americas.

It is important to look at the foundation of the dualism of Christian and heathen to comprehend the future ethos and grammar of the religion of white supremacy. This dualism became ever more important as it moved across the Atlantic Ocean with Christopher Columbus and later European explorers. It is foundational to the modern conception of persons and the development of an ordered society with Euro-Christians at the center and all others revolving around the periphery. To understand the epistemology of whiteness, one must first begin with the concept of "discovery." The myth of whiteness that is the basis for the religion of white supremacy is predicated on the belief in the "discovery" of the Americas in the fifteenth century by the Spanish, and later the British, Dutch, and French during the sixteenth century. The Western world system shapes itself, and the Western epistemological project puts European Christianity at the center of the modern world.

The word "discovery" is innocuous enough and simply means "finding something new." People discover new things every day, but in this situation the Western world is claiming to have found a whole new corner of the globe. The world, as such, is something that in this instance becomes significant in the myth of Western-led modernity. As Christopher Columbus, whose discovery is honored every year in the United States, set foot on the shores of Hispaniola, a New World paradigm started to form in which the Spanish—and later the British, Dutch, French, and Portuguese, among others—traversed the globe in search of "new" lands to claim.

In this line of thinking, discovery means much more than finding something new; rather, these discoverers proclaimed ownership of these places, including every inch of the Americas and, over the next 400+ years, the vast majority of the world. This delineation of epistemology privileges the mythology of whiteness that purports a discovery of the Americas, but why is the "discovery" of the Americas integral to the religion of white supremacy, particularly when societies and cultural systems were vast and widespread throughout the lands of the European colonial exploration for centuries before Europeans dreamed of lands to the West?[4] The Western claims of discovery instituted a modern epistemology that expanded the European understanding of the world beyond the ancient lands of Africa, Asia, and Europe.

In 1492, under the auspices of the Spanish crown and for the purposes of material and spiritual accumulation, Christopher Columbus sailed West to find a new passage to the Indian subcontinent. What he encountered after being at sea for two months changed the course of history. Columbus's, and subsequent explorers', travels to the Americas forever altered the destiny of countless persons throughout the globe. The colonizing mission of countries like France, Great Britain, and Spain, among others, redefined the ways in which the body operated in civilization, and therefore, as Enrique Dussel argues, created the modern world.[5] This "New World" created through colonization reconfigured "old world" operative motifs that in the first decades of exploration needed defining.

During the decades that Spain conquered Mexico and Peru, a debate raged within Catholic Spain to establish the rights of the indigenous populations and, based on these rights, how the Spanish empire in the Americas was permitted to treat these encountered peoples. A common notion among the Spanish people during these decades is attributable to the accounts of explorers, like Hernán Cortés and Bernal Díaz, who used their histories of conquest to portray the indigenous population as barbaric in nature and thus requiring subdual, through war and servitude to the Spanish, to condition them for the civilizing salvation of Christianity.

To make the argument for war against the peoples of the Americas, proponents of colonization developed an argument based on theology and Aristotle.[6] Arguably the most formidable scholar justifying the war and slavery of native peoples was Juan Ginés de Sepúlveda, who was trained in theology and was one of the most reputable scholars of Aristotle during the time of conquest. He employed the philosophy of Aristotle to argue that the people of Spanish America were barbaric, ignorant, and unreasoning, and that due to these facts, it was natural for these people to submit to the wiser and superior Spanish.

Another perspective took shape within Catholic Spain that is famously attributed to the friar Bartolomé de las Casas, who from the time of the early conquests witnessed firsthand the imperial treatment of the indigenous peoples. Through works like *In Defense of the Indians* and *A Brief Account of the Destruction of the Indians*, las Casas made the Spanish kingdom aware of the plight of the different peoples of the Americas under the rule of the Spanish. With his differing theological viewpoint from Sepúlveda and the Conquistadors, las Casas set upon changing the approach of the Spanish empire toward conquest and the treatment of the encountered people. Their debate was unique to the Western world until the movement to end slavery during the nineteenth century; therefore, I argue that it set the precedence for the Western worldview of non-Westerners, and for the purpose of this project, the American approach toward race and racism.[7]

In 1550, the town of Valladolid, Spain, held a theological debate commissioned by Emperor Charles V between las Casas and Sepúlveda to decide the earthly and divine rights of the indigenous peoples. Luis Rivera argues in *A Violent Evangelism: The Political and Religious Conquest of the Americas* that the debate can be understood as an argument over the correct interpretation of the papal bulls by Pope Alexander VI that established authority over new lands encountered by Catholic empires.[8] The multiple interpretations of Alexander's bulls made it necessary for Charles V to order the theological debate between las Casas and Sepúlveda to determine the ethical implications of the conquest of the Americas and whether these imperial actions were just under natural and divine law. While the council that presided over the debate at Valladolid never came to a formal conclusion, the arguments by las Casas and Sepúlveda provide significant insight into the ways in which the early modern world sought to develop an understanding of the Other and how this New Worldview became determinative in future interactions with non-Western (white) persons.

The essence of Sepúlveda's argument was that the indigenous peoples of the Americas were incapable of self-governance in several different ways, and that thus they were in need of the outside influence that the Spanish were capable of providing.[9] Sepúlveda established this argument by proposing that the Indians were "barbaric, uninstructed in letters and the art of government, completely ignorant, unreasoning, and totally incapable of learning."[10]

The use of "barbarian language" is important to Sepúlveda's argument because of how he used this term to define the relationship of the transatlantic

Other to the Spaniards.[11] The Spanish did not understand the indigenous people as subjects but rather as objects. In conceiving of the indigenous people in this way, the Spanish made the image of the encountered Other malleable to their needs. In constructing the Other, Sepúlveda determined that there were four different types of barbarians: "(1) barbarians in the proper sense of the term: are cruel and inhuman men . . . (2) barbarian secundum quid: men who do not speak the language of another people . . . (3) barbarians in the strict sense: men of inherently savage and evil instincts, incapable of governing themselves . . . [and] (4) Non-Christians."[12] Sepúlveda used these categories of barbarians to demonstrate that the indigenous Other is barbaric on many levels and, according to this logic, incapable of self-government, thus necessitating the intervention of the Spanish and the requisite submission of the Indians. He argued that in each case, the Spanish empire was just in waging war to subdue barbaric people. The accounts of Spanish conquerors made it possible to believe that Sepúlveda's classifications of barbarian fit within the situation of the Latin American conquests by describing the indigenous population as combative. The most damning charge against the indigenous people was the accusation of human sacrifice, which became a supreme justification for Bernal Díaz and Hernán Cortés during their conquest of Mexico.

In his rebuttal of Sepúlveda, las Casas refuted each claim that is made, but what is more important to understand are the effects of the theological debate. While many scholars point to las Casas as a great defender of human rights during the initial decades of European expansion, what difference did his arguments make in the trajectory of colonial expansion? Within three centuries of the debate at Valladolid, North and South America had been "settled" by Europeans, and the economy of the United States was reliant on the southern economy model of chattel slavery, and Africa and Asia had been colonized by European economic and military powers. As scholars like Robert Young have noted, las Casas is an important figure in the understanding of postcolonial works, but Enrique Dussel is right in assessing that las Casas failed to stem the tide of human exploitation. "Bartolomé de Las Casas will be known in Modernity as a political failure, although also the first critic and the most radical skeptic of the civilizing claim of Modernity."[13]

In light of las Casas's failure, the question becomes: How did the political philosophy of Sepúlveda impact the worldview of what would become Europe, specifically the European powers seeking transatlantic expansion of dominion and economic wealth? The work of Dussel is indispensable in the quest for understanding the ways in which the initial colonial worldview of Sepúlveda, among others, was determinative in the Othering of peoples throughout the world that continues in the supposed postmodern world. In *The Politics of Liberation*, Dussel sets out to create a new understanding of world history that challenges the predominately understood history constructed by the West.

The epistemological understanding of discovery can be viewed in many different ways, including the philosophical arguments of Walter Mignolo's zero point epistemology and Charles Mills's epistemology of ignorance. Mignolo asserts the centrality of European ways of knowing in direct opposition to other epistemic forms.[14] Mills's epistemology of ignorance points to the inability of whites to recognize the system created by white supremacy.[15] Both of these arguments are influential and important to comprehending the modern epistemology that began with Columbus's encounter with the people of Hispaniola. However, I argue that the advent of modern epistemology operates more through a religio-cultural myth in the vein of creation narratives, like the book of Genesis. To frame the epistemological foundation of modernity through discovery would work in the following way:

> In the beginning, the white men of Europe ventured west. After weeks of travel through vast nothingness, their vessels of exploration and trade came upon a new horizon of discovery. In adoration of God and man, the men of Britain, France, Holland, Portugal, and Spain laid claim to this new world. In honor and praise, the men set forth to proclaim the good news of their God and the benevolence of their Kings. The men of Europe professed their religion of *Pax Christendom* through civilization. The people of the new world, blinded by their superstition, failed to convert to the message of *Pax Christendom* because of their wickedness. The men of Europe used the power of their God to subdue the land and its people. The culture of Christendom, being clearly superior, proved the right of the men of Europe to rule this new land. The men of Europe, empowered by their God, set to tame this new creation. First, they moved to honor their God by naming the creatures of the land and sea and the places of this new world. They named the people heathens because they did not know the all-powerful god of Europe. The curious people of this new land, in recognition of their inferiority, submitted themselves to the men of Europe, who brought order and civility to the untamed land. In subduing the beasts of the land, the men of Europe set to honor their God through naming the new land.[16] First was Hispaniola, then America, and later New Amsterdam (New York). The men of New Christendom quickly subdued the wilderness in honor of God. The men of Europe then moved beyond the lands of New Christendom to expand the glory of God to the ends of the land. The God of Christendom was pleased with the men of Europe and saw that it was good.

The epistemology of whiteness constructed itself in such a way that Euro-Christians operated out a spatial understanding of the world. This meant that in the encounter of civilizations, Euro-Christians used the power of meaning to claim what they came to know through the act of naming.[17] The epistemic naming of the colonial project led white supremacist Christianity to the appropriation of what it had named. As a result, modernity as a way of knowing is subject to and defined by white supremacist Christianity's claim to ultimacy.[18]

The myth of the religion of white supremacy, like the sacred stories of the Abrahamic faiths, does not end with Genesis; rather, the religion of white supremacy is forever framed by its genesis myth.[19] Out of nothing came the story of creation. While the Christians of Europe solidified their power in the fifteenth century with the enforced decline of the Moors of Spain and later the Turks of the east, the epistemology of the Old World could not prepare the European psyche for the paradigm shift of discovery. This is why scholars like Mignolo and Dussel see the European encounter with the civilizations of what would become the Americas as the cosmological shift that birthed the new age of modernity.

> Mignolo's use of Zero Point Epistemology is crucial to the epistemology of discovery.
> Basically, zero point epistemology is the ultimate grounding of knowledge, which paradoxically is ungrounded, or grounded neither in geo-historical location nor in bio-graphical configurations of the bodies. The geopolitical and bio-graphic politics of knowledge is hidden in the transparency and the universality of the zero point. It is grounding without grounding; it is in the mind and not the brain and in the heart.[20]

What Mignolo is alluding to with his philosophy of zero point epistemology is the genesis of a new system of knowledge that places Europe at the center of the world. This new epistemology sets forth the claims of European superiority as found in the hegemonic power of male-gendered Christians. As agents of God, these Christian men sought to reconstruct the world with Christendom at the center economically, politically, and spiritually. In order for this New World order to take place, a new system of knowing was needed to break through the geopolitics of the post-Roman world. For a millennium, the former Roman Empire battled itself and others in a clash of many cultures and economies.[21] During this time, the clash of cultures was on the micro level of nations or peoples versus other nations or peoples and not on a macro level. This would change with the discovery, as the clash of civilizations moved from the micro to the macro. But what would become the site of this new confrontation? Many scholars recognize that the initial encounters in the Americas were defined through a theological framework that partitioned Christians from barbarians and heathens. The theo-political grounding of Christian versus non-Christian, particularly during the first century of European expansion, is not in doubt. Theology was the battleground for defining the future of expansion and the treatment of the persons found in these discovered lands. The debate between las Casas and Sepúlveda was one of many as the Christian world began to comprehend this new wrinkle in sacred history. The worldview of the city of god and the city of man was drastically reinterpreted from the Augustinian interpretation of two worlds into one cosmological world here one side sought theological supremacy.

Through this cosmological worldview, a new theological framework produced a substantively different knowledge structure. This structure is epitomized by Sepúlveda's classification of barbarians. As discussed earlier, Sepúlveda established four categories of barbarians. In essence, he argued that barbarians are cruel, incapable of speaking the language, savage, and non-Christians.[22] Under these distinctions, the Spanish came to know the people of the Americas as wholly different from themselves. Sepúlveda's construction of the barbarian enabled the people of Spain, and later the rest of Western Europe, to comprehend themselves and the people of the Americas as coming from separate worlds. In the battle between the people of God and others, Sepúlveda's argument became the normative way of knowing the people of the discovered lands. As such, the new cosmic *raison d'être* necessitated the pacification of barbarian people in the same way God called Adam to have dominion over the earth in Genesis 1:26.

The contours of the epistemology of whiteness are shaped by discovery. The influence of discovery necessitates a reading of Genesis 1:26, which grouped barbarians and wild animals together over whom humankind is to have dominion. The passage states, "Then God said, 'Let us make humankind in our image, according to our likeness and let them have dominion over the fish of the sea, and over the birds of the air, and over the cattle and over the wild animals of the earth.'" Logically, the people of Christendom were different than the people of the Americas. As Augustine sought to construct two histories after the sacking of Rome, which began a new age, so too Sepúlveda and others imagined a dualistic history at the beginning of modernity. The epistemic shift of modernity took the cosmology of two histories to signify that the people of the Americas were not fully human. The status as subhuman, or more accurately as barbarian, made the people of the Americas subjects or wards of the Christian invaders through divine fiat.

As the Christian world solidified and expanded its dominion over the Americas, another shift took place in the framing of Christendom through epistemology. Mignolo describes this epistemic shift in the following way:

> What supports the four 'heads' or interrelated spheres of management and control are the two 'legs,' that is, the racial and patriarchial foundation of knowledge . . . that the historical foundation of the colonial matrix was theological: it was Christian theology that located the distinction between Christians, Moors,

and Jews in the 'blood.' Although the quarrel between the three religions of the book had a long history, it has been reconfigured since 1492, when Christians managed to expel Moors and Jews from the peninsula and enforced conversion on those who wanted to stay. Simultaneously, the racial configuration between Spanish, Indian, and African began to take shape in the New World. By the 18th century, 'blood' as a marker of race/racism was transferred to skin. And theology was displaced by secular philosophy and sciences. The Linnaean system of classification helped the cause. Secular racism came to be based on ego-politics of knowledge; but it so happened that the agents and institutions that embodied secular ego-politics of knowledge were, like those who embodied theo-politics of knowledge, mostly white European males. So, the struggle between theologism and secularism was a family feud. Proponents of both were Christian, white, and male, and assumed heterosexual relations as the norm—consequently also classified gender distinctions and sexual normativity.[23]

While Mignolo is correct about the effect on gender and sexuality. For this argument, it is more important to focus on the relationship of the theological and secular interpretations of race/racism. In addition to Mignolo, many scholars delineate the arguments of racism as first being theological and then later on secular reason. Certainly, this is true in a strict dichotomy of faith and reason as both parties like to argue in modern history. I posit that while this delineation might be formally true in the sense of intellectual history, it cannot be ignored that theo-politics framed the epistemological realities of discovery. But is that where theology left the equation? Unequivocally speaking, that is not the case.

Mignolo frames the struggle of theologism and secularism as a "family feud," and history supports this distinction. I contend that the secular and philosophical language of racism and white supremacy is still the same coding as theology. Secularism rewrote the A+B=C equation of theology as 1+2=3. They seem like different equations, but in fact all that changed is the symbolic makeup of the equation, not the symbolic nature of the equation. In the epistemology of white supremacy, both equations signify the superiority of white bodies over and against nonwhite bodies, but the wording changed. The changing of the language or grammar of racism leads to seemingly disparate results, yet in actuality, when the actions are reduced to their code, the result is the same. For this reason, I propose the epistemology of whiteness to describe the orders of knowing that define modernity. This means that the epistemology of whiteness is determinative in how people understand and operate within modern American culture.

The case for the epistemology of whiteness moves beyond the influence of discovery to encompass the progression of the orders of knowing beyond the initial dichotomy of Christian and barbarian/heathen, while recognizing that modernity as we know it would not without this dichotomy even if the terms

have changed. This line of thinking is proven by the passage of the Naturalization Act of 1790, as discussed in chapter 5. Mignolo and others argue
that the shift to secularism took place during the eighteenth century, and
that therefore, the Naturalization Act is a product of secular racism. The law
states, "any alien, being a free white person . . . may be admitted to become a
citizen thereof."[24] Clearly, the language of the law is different from that which
Sepúlveda used 240 years earlier to classify the people of the Americas. The
symbols of the equation have changed from barbarian to nonwhite, but the
crux is the same in both ways of knowing.

The idea of citizenship being available to white persons is straightforward
enough and shows the preference of skin color over a religio-cultural classification of Christian, but this does not mean that Sepúlveda and the 1790
act are completely different. The 1790 law's true meaning was unveiled in
the Supreme Court of the United States (SCOTUS) cases on immigration, in
particular the decisions in *Takao Ozawa v. United States* and *United States v.
Bhagat Singh Thind*. These decisions established a bait and switch precedent
of whiteness that breaks down a strict separation of theology and secularism
that lends itself to theologism.[25] Ozawa was denied citizenship because he
was not scientifically white, which lent itself to Thind's case. As Thind met
the scientific coding of whiteness, he should have retained his certificate of
naturalization, but that was not the case. Instead, the court rescinded his certificate based on his unsuitability for the responsibility of citizenship. This is
pivotal to deconstructing the secular equation.

The order of knowing employed in 1923 by SCOTUS established a baseline of whiteness on the basis of civilized versus uncivilized, in the same
way as President Jackson justified the removal of indigenous people from the
American South. What becomes apparent in the *Thind* case is an inseparable
quality of Christianity, citizenship, and whiteness. Legally speaking, this cannot be the case because of the First Amendment to the U.S. Constitution. And
yet, the First Amendment did not deter the SCOTUS from pointing to Thind's
racial status as justification for revoking his citizenship claim. Ultimately,
the argument against Thind rested on his status as non-Christian—as such,
he could never belong to the Christian realm. In this sense, the epistemology of whiteness returns to a divine understanding of history. The world of
Christianity, that is, of whiteness, was ordained by God to have dominion.
To this extent, the world of non-Christians, that is, the nonwhite, is beyond
the pale of God and is left to God's chosen people to control. To accept
nonmembers into the community would be an abomination against God and
God's command.

The epistemology of whiteness instilled into the divine community a
knowledge of superiority that eternally connected the people of God. This
sacred connection with God acted as a powerful signifier to one's relationship

with the divine that grew into something different entirely through the embodiment of whiteness. The drive to define the relationship between the British (and later the United States) and other people in the lands that would become the United States framed what would become an ontological embracing of white supremacy. The embodiment of this particular mixture of Christianity and white supremacy expanded the epistemology of whiteness. This does not mean that the epistemological framework ceased to be relevant as white supremacist Christianity became something that defined a person's being. Without the epistemology of whiteness, the assurance of superiority would be diminished. For this reason, the myths of Americanness and the sacred version of American history are indispensable in the continued maintenance of an embodied white supremacy. As Thandeka argues in *Learning to be White*, belief in white supremacist Christianity is something that whites are not born with, but rather something that they learn through socialization.[26] This process involves a particular form of teaching that is taught in many different settings including the school and the home.

The teaching of white supremacist Christianity acts as a catechetical rite of passage into the larger society. Young whites are taught the system of beliefs to the extent that the lessons become a part, not only of their way of knowing, but of the ways in which they find meaning. In finding meaning through the lens of white supremacist Christianity, a paradigm of ultimacy is introduced into the equation. The belief in a particular form of American history that is shaped more by myth than historical fact enables whites to find ultimacy in who they are. The ultimacy found in this construction is not necessarily in the shape of hyperpatriotism, but rather in the shape of something that connects them to the history of greatness. Members of the white supremacist faith find their drive to ultimacy in their belief that their whiteness connects them to the numinous white supremacy that has led America to greatness.

In the historical narrative as viewed through the distorted lens of the epistemology of whiteness, the god of white supremacy prevailed over the indigenous heathens to ensure that only whites inhabited the land destined by god. Their god provided African bodies to ensure that whites in the new land would prosper. Even after the war to end slavery, whites came together through their common belief in white supremacist Christianity to safeguard the country against the cosmic assault that blackness would bring to society.[27] The power of ultimacy found in white flesh made it impossible for whites to permit any sort of blemish in the land of the God of white supremacy. While nonwhites continued to receive new forms of freedom in the United States through the adjudication of the legal system, white supremacist Christianity constructed new ways of maintaining white superiority. The drive of "against-each-otherness," as described in Tillich's theology of the ultimacy of the god of space, operated by taking events that could devalue the God of white supremacy and using them to create new barriers to safeguard the powers and purity of whiteness.[28]

THE ONTOLOGY OF WHITE SUPREMACY

To start delineating the premise of white supremacy having an ontological character, I want to do what George Yancy calls "look, a White!"[29] Of course, the phrase is a turn on the white supremacist idea of "look, a Negro!"[30] Whites historically used this phrasing as a fight-or-flight response to alert the body of the imminent threat posed by a black body. While most whites do not explicitly use the phrase "look, a Negro!" in the contemporary context, the concept is still an ontological marker for blackness. In an instance, one that was put in motion centuries ago and will move into the future, the location of black space became a direct threat to sacred white space. Yancy turns this ontological process on its head in order to see white bodies as also marked.

> The act of marking whiteness, then, is itself an act of historicizing whiteness, an act of situating whiteness within the context of material forces and race interest-laden values that reinforce whiteness as a site of privilege and hegemony. Marking whiteness is about exposing the ways in which whites have created a form of "humanism" that obfuscates their hegemonic efforts to treat their experiences as universal and representative.[31]

Turning white supremacy into a category of investigation removes its ability to hide in society. As Yancy would say, "look, a White!" The purpose of the chapters to follow is to actively mark moments of white supremacy. By marking how white supremacy works, I show the ontological nature of its inner workings in white people. Just like how Yancy argues that "look, a Negro!" ontologically marks black space that threatens white space, "look, a White!" signifies the possible threat of white space.

The system of white supremacy relies on the inability of whites to mark white space. While nonwhites can easily mark this space because of its continual transgressions, whites do not, and often cannot, see these transgressions due to the normativity of whiteness within U.S. culture. To mark white supremacy means to also define it and to confirm its existence. In marking, the beliefs of colorblindness are called directly into question, as white people cannot be both colorblind and white supremacist. Charles Mills points to the fact of whites being white supremacist in this way: "The idea of white supremacy is intended in part to capture the crucial reality that *normal* workings of the social system continue to disadvantage blacks in large measure *independently* of racist feelings."[32] Mills substantiates the point made previously that this work is not about the Klan or other organized or individual forces of intentional racism. Yancy furthers this by calling into question the myth of "good whites" and "bad whites."[33] White people seek to deflect claims of white supremacy or racism as the "problem" of others, and yet this is precisely an act of white supremacy. Disavowing one's claim to white space with statements like "I have black friends" or "I don't see race" is an act of Yancy's "social ontology of whiteness."[34]

The social ontology of whiteness makes possible the dualism of the good and bad white person. While I connect the problem more to the place of white supremacy than whiteness due to white supremacy's nexus as a power structure, it is clear that Yancy is showing how whiteness in its traditional mode operates in an "us versus them" mode.[35] It pits whites against blacks by constructing the essence of blackness as a threat to white space, and it creates the false dualism of good and bad whites. During the research for this book, I came upon this very problem of good versus bad whites in an innocuous conversation with other theologians. While sitting at a local coffee shop, I overheard two professors from a local university discussing their respective religion courses. As a good graduate student, I sheepishly walked over to introduce myself to future colleagues. Both were white men who took a moment to speak to me and ask about my dissertation. I described my project and expected possible questions, but instead received a comment with an aura of confidence that I must see a bunch of interesting tattoos in my research.

As we said our pleasantries and I walked away from their table, I was left with the feeling of confusion. Why would these professors of religion shrug off my work by talking about tattoos? I had made the obvious connection to them referencing skinheads, but I clearly stated my project was about how white supremacy influences society. I later realized that these white men did not see themselves as white. They could not see beyond the history of "bad" white persons who had personally owned slaves, held the batons, or unleashed the dogs. They were "good" colorblind Americans who lived their lives free of any messiness such as race. And yet, these men carried out the performance of white supremacy just in their response, through deflection. "By perpetuating the dualism between the 'good white' and the 'bad white,' whites attempt to mute the claim that white racism is not limited to the KKK, neo-Nazi skinheads, White Aryan Resistance, and other white racist groups."[36] The professors fell into the trap of assuming their own whiteness by denying its existence. Obviously, these two professors are not the focus of this work. What they do show is how the social ontology of whiteness enables itself to continue and subsist in a time without formal legalized white supremacy. What they did show is how white supremacy inhabits its own space as superior to others. This is nowhere more apparent than in the refusal to see white supremacy as only the purview of skinheads.[37]

The ontology of white supremacy operates by ensuring the preservation of white space. This is seen in chapter 4 by the organization of whites in different geographies seeking to fulfill the same goal of preserving their sacred space as God's chosen people. In each case—Tulsa, Marion, and Detroit—the white people rally around their own specialness as recipients of white space. Yancy's social ontology of whiteness leads to the natural conclusion that there must be something binding whites together in a common spatiality. It is necessary to take the social ontology of whiteness to the next level and honestly say it is indeed a contract as Charles Mills understands it. "But the peculiar contract to which I am referring, though based on the social contract tradition that has been central to Western political theory, is not a contract between everybody ('we the people'), but between just the people who count, the people who really are people ('we the white people'). So it is a Racial Contract."[38] Mills's idea of the Racial Contract takes the ontology of white supremacy to its necessary seat of power as more than just a commonality between white folks, whether "good" or "bad," and shows the fact of universal participation.

As noted earlier, white supremacy is a god of space, and this space must always be preserved as white space. For most of modernity, accomplishing the preservation of white space was done through domination. The British and later the United States used physical power to kill, manipulate, and control nonwhite bodies in white space. The more power accumulated by white supremacy, the more whites benefited from their place at the top of the chain of being. The white god was good to white people by ensuring that they operated in an exclusive manner above nonwhite bodies. The bond of white supremacy not only preserved white space in the United States, but also made possible the full exploitation of nonwhite bodies which happened to be trespassing on literal white space or were brought to the United States. The ultimate power subsumed through formalized white supremacy created the myth of ultimacy as found in white space. White supremacy became more than just a place of white transcendence. "Whiteness is true transcendence, an ecstatic mode of being; blackness, however, in its ontological structure, is true immanence, a thing unable to be other than what it was born to be, a thing closed upon itself, locked into an ontological realm where things exist not 'for-themselves' but 'in-themselves,' waiting to be ordered by some external, subjugating purposive (white) consciousness."[39] During the time of legislative white supremacy, the formalization of white supremacy as a religion became natural due to the power of white space. This power enabled whites to control their own destiny not just individually (where some clearly benefit more than most) but also through controlling the destiny of nonwhite bodies. White supremacy controlled the personhood of everyone within its grasp, which on a large scale meant the vast majority of the world through

Euro-U.S. imperialism. And yet, this was different in the United States. White rule began from the moment the Puritans and other British colonists claimed divine right to the land. The east coast became, both in the sense of land and theologically, white space. From that moment forward until the 1960s, white supremacist Christianity wielded the power of the white God through law.

This also made it possible for whites to use extralegal means, for example race riots and lynching, to ensure their place within the hierarchy of beings within the United States, while at the same time, the federal government ensured the purity of white space, for example through the Federal Housing Authority. For these power dynamics to work, whites had to understand their place within the world through transcendence. White space must be a space of sacred worth. This could not be possible through simply an epistemological lens. To know oneself to be special is one thing, but for white supremacy to work, this knowledge had to become a part of the operational realities of society. Whiteness had to signify specialness and power for whites and against nonwhites. This is why John H. McClendon states ontology is important to the idea of race.

> Race as a social category is ontologically valid and true, if and when our starting point is material relations of production. The material reality of race as a social category does not require an appeal to nature, natural science, or biology. Just as value, a political economics category, is not rooted in any state of nature but instead in a given set of social relations of production. Yet race and value both possess definitive forms in materially determinate sets of social relations.[40]

This becomes important when we look to the specialness of white space. During and after the formalized white supremacy era in the United States, the ultimacy of whiteness continued. It most certainly changed, but its material value as a space of transcendence to whites never ceased. The social relations among whites and nonwhites has legally shifted from "we the white people" to "we the people," and yet, socially speaking, the ontology of white supremacy still places whites at the top of the hierarchy of social relations. Whites still hold the money and the government in ways that could never really be overturned. This is where the idea of contract becomes a part of the white supremacist Christianity. While formally the United States is not a nation of legal white supremacy, the centuries of legalization established a social reality of white space that adheres to moral coding, not laws. White supremacy is more than laws; it is a special idea that controls the fabric of white space.[41]

The history of the United States is told from the perspective of white supremacist Christianity as it finds ultimacy in its god. From the "discovery" of the Americas to the mythology of the United States as a Christian nation, the story is told through a lens of whiteness. The ontology of white supremacy uses this history to construct a religious motif where whiteness takes on a divine character. This ontology transforms the epistemology of whiteness from a system where Christians are superior to non-Christians because of their perceived civilized character to one where non-Christians, that is, nonwhites, are deficient in their essence.

The historical vignettes of part two build on each other to shape a society where whiteness has attained ultimate meaning. This conversion embodies the drive for ultimacy by giving meaning to whites in the United States while at the same time condemning nonwhites because of their place beyond redemption by the God of white supremacy. In the next chapter, I show how the image of the white Christ comes to be the lynchpin in this faith system. Thus far, this project has described a foundation of a white supremacist Christianity through the analysis of epistemology and ontology, but with the image of the white Christ, the symbolization of white supremacist Christianity reveals the distortion of the Christian faith in the United States.

NOTES

1. "Romney Jokes about His Birth Certificate; Obama Campaign Accuses Him of Embracing 'Birtherism,'" *Washington Post*, August 24, 2012, accessed on February 13, 2015, http://www.washingtonpost.com/politics/romney-jokes-about-his-birth-certificate-obama-campaign-accuses-him-of-embracing-birtherism/2012/08/24/bda35810-ee14–11e1-b0eb-dac6b50187ad_story.html.

2. "Donald Trump 'Birther' Remarks Take Centre Stage," *Guardian*, May 29, 2012, accessed February 13, 2015, http://www.theguardian.com/world/2012/may/29/mitt-romney-donald-trump-live.

3. Roediger, 13.

4. For more information, see Howard Zinn, *A People's History of the United States* (New York: Harper Collins, 2010), 17–22.

5. Enrique Dussel, *Invention of the Americas: Eclipse of "the Other" and the Myth of Modernity*, trans. by Michael D. Barber (New York: Continuum, 1995), 26.

6. Ibid., 28.

7. The idea of non-Westerners is constructed out of the need to establish what it meant to be civilized. The connection of civilized to Christianity by Sepúlveda and others has manifested itself through different language over the past five centuries. In each iteration the framework remains the same: something about those who are Christian, European, or white makes them superior to those who are not. The key denominator is not something one group did to make itself superior, but rather that they are superior because of who they are.

8. Luis Rivera, *A Violent Evangelism: The Political and Religious Conquest of the Americas* (Louisville: Westminster John Knox Press, 1992), 31.

9. It is important to note that the most succinct account of Sepúlveda's argument is made by las Casas in his *In Defense of the Indians*. This means that the following

description is generally the argument of Sepúlveda, but it must also be remembered that it is presented by someone who is invested in discrediting this particular worldview.

10. Bartolomé de las Casas, *In Defense of the Indians*, ed. and trans. by Stafford Poole (Dekalb, IL: Northern Illinois University Press, 1992), 11.

11. Tzvetan Todorov, *The Conquest of the America: The Question of the Other*, trans. by Richard Howard (New York: Harper Perennial, 1984), 49.

12. Angel Losada, "The Controversy Between Sepúlveda and Las Casas in the Junta of Valladolid," in *Bartolomé de las Casas in History: Toward an Understanding of the Man and His Work*, ed. by Juan Friede and Benjamin Keen (Dekalb, IL: Northern Illinois University Press, 1971), 284–5.

13. Enrique Dussel, *The Politics of Liberation: A Critical World History* (New York: SCM Press, 2011), 206.

14. Walter Mignolo, *The Darker Side of Western Modernity: Global Futures, Decolonial Options* (Durham: Duke University Press, 2011), 80.

15. Charles W. Mills, *The Racial Contract* (Ithaca, NY: Cornell University Press, 1997), 18.

16. Tzvetan Todorov, *The Conquest of America: The Question of the Other*. Trans. by Richard Howard (New York: Harper & Row, 1984), 27.

17. Ibid., 28.

18. As the book proceeds, it is important for the reader to understand that passages which unpack the rationale of white supremacist thinking are *not* endorsements, but rather analysis.

19. The term "religion of white supremacy" is anachronistic in attaching itself to the early centuries of colonialism. The Spanish would not have considered themselves white. The term points to the idea that ultimacy is not found in Christianity; rather, it is a particular understanding of the faith. From this worldview, Christianity is connected to something else that makes simple adherence to the faith insufficient for full admittance into civilization. In later centuries, the particular form of Christianity that the colonizers envision transforms into the connection of Europeanness with Christianity. The inclusion of the United States into this dynamic initiates another manifestation that morphs Europeanness and Christianity. At this point, the religion of white supremacy becomes firmly established.

20. Walter D. Mignolo, *The Darker Side of Western Modernity: Global Futures, Decolonial Options* (Durham: Duke University Press, 2011), 80.

21. Ibid., 28.

22. Angel Losada, "The Controversy Between Sepulveda and Las Casas in the Junta of Valladolid," in *Bartolomé de las Casas in History: Toward an Understanding of the Man and His Work*, 278–307, edited by Juan Friede and Benjamin Keen (Dekalb: Northern Illinois University, 1971), 284–5.

23. Mignolo, *The Darker Side of Western Modernity: Global Futures, Decolonial Options*, 8–9.

24. An Act to Establish an Uniform Rule of Naturalization, 1st Cong., 2d sess. (March 26, 1790.)

25. This is a complicated and potentially hazardous idea. I am not using it to suggest the superiority of theology over other disciplines, but rather, the inseparableness of theology from any concepts of racism or white supremacy.

26. Thandeka, *Learning to be White: Money, Race, and God in America* (New York: Continuum, 2007), 17.

27. Edward J. Blum, *Reforging the White Republic: Race, Religion, and American Nationalism, 1865–1898* (Baton Rouge: Louisiana State University Press, 2005), 247.

28. Paul Tillich, *Theology of Culture*, edited by Robert C. Kimball (New York: Oxford University Press, 1959), 33.

29. George Yancy, *Look, a White!: Philosophical Essays on Whiteness* (Philadelphia: Temple University Press, 2012), 6.

30. Ibid., 1.

31. Ibid., 17.

32. Charles Mills, "Racial Exploitation and the Wages of Whiteness," in *What White Looks Like: African-American Philosophers on the Whiteness Question*, edited by George Yancy (New York: Routledge, 2004), 31.

33. George Yancy, "Introduction: Fragments of a Social Ontology of Whiteness," in *What White Looks Like: African-American Philosophers on the Whiteness Question*, edited by George Yancy (New York: Routledge, 2004), 4.

34. Ibid., 5.

35. John H. McClendon, "On the Nature of Whiteness and the Ontology of Race: Toward a Dialectical Materialist Analysis," in *What White Looks Like: African-American Philosophers on the Whiteness Question*, edited by George Yancy (New York: Routledge, 2004), 223.

36. Yancy, "Introduction: Fragments of a Social Ontology of Whiteness," 4.

37. Ibid., 13.

38. Mills, "Racial Exploitation and the Wages of Whiteness," 3.

39. Yancy, "Introduction: Fragments of a Social Ontology of Whiteness," 11.

40. McClendon, "On the Nature of Whiteness and the Ontology of Race," 216.

41. Mills, "Racial Exploitation and the Wages of Whiteness," 31.

Chapter 2

The White Christ

What follows in this chapter is the formulation of the soteriology of white flesh. This chapter argues that with Sallman's *Head of Christ*, as a cultural fulcrum, created a form of Christianity that is dependent on the myths of white supremacy to maintain and recreate itself. This chapter argues that the history of the United States created a cultural form of Christianity that is dependent on the myths of white supremacy to maintain and recreate itself. This chapter will proceed by deconstructing the soteriology of white flesh and how U.S. history made this possible. The second part of the chapter will demonstrate, through the work of Paul Tillich, why this iteration of Christianity in the United States operates as a demonic interpretation of the faith. Finally, I return to Warner Sallman's *Head of Christ* as a symbol of white supremacist Christianity and how this image, as a model of religious expression, is more than a painting.

In the previous chapter, I demonstrated how the history of the U.S. and Euro-Christian colonization shaped an epistemology of whiteness and how it further developed into an ontology of white supremacy. This line of thinking revealed how the colonial thinkers framed their worldview through the cosmic understanding of Christian and non-Christian in order to come to terms with the radical reorientation of their world. The "discovery" of the Americas provided a new opportunity to spread the Christian understanding of civilization and the expansion of Christian economic prospects. In North America, the creation of the epistemology of whiteness, which should be read as Euro-Christian, shaped future interactions between Euro-Christians and people that were known as heathens. The epistemic argument gave rise to the justification for Euro-Christians to claim North America through the power of naming and military force.

SOTERIOLOGY OF WHITE FLESH

The New World became a place for Christians to shape their destiny outside the shadow of the Moors to the south and east. This "New World" was to be the Christian world where God ruled through the divine mandate given to the Euro-Christian settlers. Through this mandate, Euro-Christians set up their "New World" in their image; while conversion was initially a hope throughout the Americas, the Euro-Christian settlers, particularly in British North America, abandoned these ideas. In a theological shift, the British settlers transitioned from a knowledge of Euro-Christian superiority to the ontology of white supremacy.

The move from an epistemic worldview to an ontic one changed the trajectory of the colonies that would become the United States. No longer was the drive of conversion a necessary component of the colonizing mission. With the shift to an ontological understanding of superiority, the Euro-Christians, and later U.S. Christians, the theological underpinnings became one of cosmic destiny.[1] Indigenous people and Africans could convert to Christianity under the rule of whites, but unlike before, this conversion could not change the barbarity of their being. The hereditariness of the ontology of white supremacy instilled permanence to the equation of Christian superiority. As Rebecca Goetz shows in *The Baptism of Early Virginia*[2], the colonists came to understand their whiteness through a theological motif. No longer was confessional Christianity a part of the equation in the British colonies and later in the United States.

To be born black meant to always be black, and to be born an Indian meant always to be an Indian. To put it another way, the biological destiny of birth confirmed the theological destiny of life.[3] This theological destiny justified the shift to chattel slavery and the removal of the Five Civilized Nations from the southern states through the infamous Trail of Tears. White supremacy does not end with the theological formation of the ontology of white supremacy. In fact, the religion of white supremacy would not be nearly as potent without its foundation in Christianity. The cultural embeddedness of Christianity added a further element to the formation of the religion of whiteness that shifted it to a white supremacist Christianity and built a faith system modeled on the dogmas, doctrine, and myths of Christianity, but reinterpreted through a uniquely U.S.- Christian model. Willie James Jennings and James W. Perkinson are particularly helpful in understanding how a soteriology of white flesh is embedded within the Euro-Christian model and later the U.S.-Christian model.

In *The Christian Imagination: Theology and the Origins of Race*, Willie Jennings seeks to show how the colonizing experience shaped the modern construction of race. Unlike other constructions of race, Jennings places modern racism within the Christian worldview. This is particularly important for comprehending the use of soteriology as a definitive marker of white supremacy as it relates to Christianity. Jennings argues that from the outset of colonial exploration, those who partook in colonization envisioned their work in soteriological terms. This vision was particularly important for Christopher Columbus.[4] In leaving the Christian world of Europe, the explorers entered a world where their Christianness was not a given trait among those they encountered. This resulted in the Christians embodying their Christianity as something that was definitive about themselves, and as a result, the bodies the explorers encountered also took on significance.[5] These encounters led the explorers to seek a theological system that could comprehend this radically different world from the one they had left.

The creation of the white/nonwhite binary helped shape this New World theology, but as Jennings argues, it took theologians, like Alessandro Valignano (1539–1601), to recreate Christian theology in light of "discovery" to provide a Christian model that could explain why Christians were superior to the people of the Americas.[6] Valignano constructed this theological reasoning through a rereading of Israel as God's chosen people. The chosenness of Israel was replaced in the work of Valignano and other theologians with Christianity. In this theological model, the people of Israel are no longer God's chosen people and are replaced through the concept of supersessionism by Christianity. In subverting the claim of Israel, this new Christian supersessionism superseded Judaism for the chosenness of God's people. But Israel was more than a religious system. The concept of Israel was a collection of people with a common religio-cultural system, whereas Christianity was a religious system to which many different cultural groups adhered throughout the land that would eventually be called Europe.

The cultural void the new Christian supersessionism created required the creation of a new identity in the form of Europeanness.

Such a suspicion and fear indicated a profound theological distortion. Here was a process of discerning Christian identity that, because it had jettisoned Israel from its calculus of the formation of Christian life, created a conceptual vacuum that was filled by the European. But not simply qua European; rather the very process of becoming Christian took on new ontic markers. Those markers of being were aesthetic and racial. This was not a straightforward matter of replacement and now theological reconfiguration. European Christians reconfigured the vision of God's attention and love for Israel, that is, they reconfigured a vision of Israel's election. If Israel had been the visibly elect of God, then that visibility in the European imagination migrated without return to a new home shaped now by new visual markers. If Israel's election had been the compass around which Christian identity gained its bearings and found its trajectory, now with this reconfiguration the body of the European would be the compass marking divine election. More importantly, that new elected body, the white body, would be a discerning body, able to detect holy effects and saving grace. Valignano performs this new reconfigured vision of election precisely in the discernment of racial being.[7]

The language of election is important to fully understanding how the shift was made to a white supremacist Christianity, from the standpoint of precolonial Christianity to one where coloniality necessitated a change. With the coding of election, the colonial system becomes a system of God's people juxtaposed with the nonelect.[8] Election enables the moves from epistemology, where the people of Europe see this new group in the Americas and know they are different, to explaining the difference in terms of the elected embodiment of God within the Euro-Christians, instead of Israel, through a codified theological modernity. The shift to theological modernity accompanied other forms of modernity in placing power of the new age in Euro-Christians. Where this modernity is different is the cosmic language of theology that altered Christianity. The compass imagery from Jennings demonstrates how the election of Euro-Christians dramatically altered the theological landscape by subverting the place of Israel as the religio-cultural marker of God. The new theological modernity stripped the Jews of their place and recast God's favor as the election of Euro-Christians.[9]

THE MARK OF THE WHITE CHRIST

The new markers of Euro-Christians must be found in some aspect of the religio-cultural makeup of white supremacist Christianity's shape. In this way, the white body becomes the new compass of Christianity and of the theological modernity as shaped by colonization. In the soteriology of the white body, grace and salvation become inscribed into particular bodies, instead as a theological marker attainable by anyone who converts to Christianity. "In the age of discovery and conquest supersessionist thinking burrowed deeply inside the logic of whiteness in a new, more sophisticated, concealed form. Indeed, supersessionist thinking is the womb in which whiteness will mature."[10] The soteriologicalness of whiteness takes shape in the birth pangs of modernity. Theological modernity is defined by its adherence to supersessionism. The ultimacy of whiteness is determinative in the category of chosenness. To be white signifies one's connection to God. On the other hand, the reality of being nonwhite leaves one vulnerable due to a detachment from God. Theological modernity finds ultimacy in the revelatory nature of whiteness. In this way, whiteness acts through the power of divine fiat.

The logic of a soteriology of white flesh might have its foundation in the annals of colonization, but the connection of white supremacy and

Christianity did not cease 300 years ago. The ability of white supremacy and Christianity to adapt with the changes in society makes the connection sustainable throughout modernity. Again, as Mignolo argues, in moving out of the early age of colonization, scholars shift from the importance of theological formation to a more scientific or philosophical view of racism. In the nineteenth century, the maintenance of racism and white supremacy becomes a matter of philosophy and science. But this cannot be fully possible when the whole rationale of coloniality, and thereby of chattel slavery and the removal of indigenous peoples, is predicated on theological markings, particularly Christianity. This demarcation of theology from philosophy and science denies the religiosity of claims made in the age of reason. Philosophy and science set out to prove that whites were superior to nonwhites in more quantifiable means, but their measures were used to prove a Truth statement that already existed. In other words, the work of philosophy and science set out to prove the preexisting answers to their work. The work of inquiry is supposed to lead to answers. Yes, science has a hypothesis in the same way other disciplines use the hypothesis model, but the supposed difference is science's use of evidence gathering techniques to either substantiate the claim or prove it wrong. The science of race did not work in this manner.

> The rise of white supremacy as an 'object of [scientific] discourse in the West' traces its genealogy to the very 'structure of modern discourse *at its inception*,' according to West. White supremacy is not simply determined by, but is constitutive of, the *episteme* of modernity. It finds its epistemological home in a set of mutually ramifying discourses that are entirely incapable of even 'fielding' the idea of black equality.[11]

Science used its models of inquiry to confirm an already-held belief in white superiority. For this reason, the work of science to prove white supremacy was not science; rather, it was further constructing the theological modernity of white supremacist Christianity. It was not the work of science because of the abandonment of the scientific method's use of unbiased experimentation to reach a conclusion. What took place through the use of the scientific method is the work of the epistemology of whiteness. The ability to know, name, and appropriate established a system in which the categories of knowing became realized and correct. The drive of science became to confirm the epistemic answers of white supremacist Christianity.

The reader might concede that the sciences did not hold to the work of pure research in the search for proof to white superiority, but does this mean that the work of science was theological? Surely, science is not and can never be theological. Herein lies the problem of scholars demarcating the theological origins of race, racism, and white supremacy from their manifestations in the nineteenth century onwards from the contemporary realities. The proposals of white supremacy and racism are Truth claims of a religious system. White supremacy is a religious system because of its meaning-making abilities within a cultural setting. This means that white supremacy has the ability to become a place of ultimacy within a religio-cultural context.

> If we specify salvation as given society's 'intimations of ultimacy' glimpsed in the way it images human wholeness for itself (as those images show up in its symbolic codes, its community structures, and its ritual expressions), and *soteriology* as both society's discourse on, and its drive for, the absolute (i.e., as both its discursive *logos* and its 'logic of practice'). We can indeed trace soteriological currents in modernity . . . which is to say, I want to understand soteriology very broadly here, as any (political) logic that discursively legitimizes a choice to risk the 'human absolute'—the suffering (or causing) of death—for the sake of the preservation or accomplishment of a pure or whole identity.[12]

Perkinson links the religio-culturalness of the soteriology of white flesh to the polis of the secular by connecting the similarities of the two through language. The political economy of white supremacy connects to the religious in Christianity by the project of theological modernity. Humanity finds its completion in the image of salvation through whiteness. This connection enables the Western world, as understood through Euro-Christianity and U.S. Christianity, to reimagine the world through a white-centric lens that provides credence to the colonial project.

The ultimacy of whiteness, as a reconfiguration of Christianity, provides the foundation for viewing the interactions between whites and nonwhites in cosmic terms. The theologicalness of white supremacist Christianity created a religio-political praxis that sprung out of the colonizing of the Americas and proceeded into the colonizing of the world. This practice did not end with the death throes of World War II. The collapse of Europe after World War II made it necessary to reinvent modernity (i.e. colonialism) in new ways because Europe did not have the resources to control the globe through military exploitation. The simple lack of military force to physically impose a white will did not mean the end of modernity; rather, it means modernity and the theology of white supremacy changed. White money now controls the world and continues to impose a white supremacist Christianity by controlling the purse strings. The countries and people that once were forced through military might to produce goods for Euro-Christians are still colonized, but it is through Western money. White supremacist Christianity holds the destiny of the world by connecting whiteness to holiness in order to place itself as the indelible marker of power in the modern world. The heresy of white supremacist Christianity is held within its resolve to itself. As Du Bois wrote,

Everything considered, the title of the universe claimed by White Folk is faulty. It ought, at least, to look plausible. How easy, then, by emphasis and omission to make children believe that every great soul the world ever saw was a white man's soul; that every great thought the world ever knew was a white man's thought—every great deed the world ever did was a white man's deed; that every great dream the world ever sang was a white man's dream.[13]

Du Bois brings this project back to the history of the United States. History enables white supremacist Christianity to present the United States as a unilateral white project. In other words, the country's narrative begins with the Pilgrims; it is founded by whites, built by whites, maintained by whites, and protected by whites. Never mind that neither the Pilgrims nor any other colonists would have survived a year without the generosity of the indigenous population, that Washington, D.C. and its monuments to white men were built by African slaves, that Africans and Indians fought for the Continental Army, that slavery enabled the U.S. economy to grow, that nonwhites from all over the world helped expand the country westward, and finally that nonwhite men and women have served the United States in many capacities as civic leaders. If these realities are discussed in the history of the United States, it is primarily through the eradication of slavery, the Civil Rights Movement, or the election of President Barack Obama. The history of nonwhites is sequestered to these periods of time.

U.S. history, as written for mass consumption, is more than a collection of dates and facts; rather, it operates as a canon and provides a great deal of meaning for white supremacist Christianity. For this reason, politicians find the presentation of history in the educational system to be a necessary topic of discussion, even going so far as to remove Thomas Jefferson, the main writer of the Declaration of Independence, from the curriculum due to his inability to fit the national narrative.[14]

As Du Bois argued in "The Souls of White Folk," "a nation's religion is its life, and as such white Christianity is a miserable failure."[15] A century ago, Du Bois recognized the connection between the U.S. nation and Christianity. As a religious system, there is nothing in the character of the nation that can be left to chance in terms of contradicting the overall narrative. Indeed, the United States has nonwhite national figures—as demonstrated by the monument in honor of Martin Luther King, Jr. just off the National Mall in Washington, D.C.—but if one looks at the narrative arc of U.S. history, it is one of whiteness.

In constructing the religious components of white supremacist Christianity, one could argue that what has been described is merely ideology. Certainly, many disciplines may argue that whiteness or white supremacy is an ideology, but this line of thinking does not fully comprehend the complexity of how white supremacist Christianity operates. It is the interweaving of white supremacy and Christianity as cultural marker that makes possible its drive for ultimacy. George Kelsey, in *Racism and the Christian Understanding of Man,* succinctly states it as, "Racism is a faith. It is a form of idolatry."[16] To understand the concept of white supremacy as a religious belief, particularly in connection to Christianity, leads to questions of how it could be interpreted this way. Returning to Paul Tillich, religion must be comprehended in a very different sense than a common observer of religion would recognize. To put it plainly, Tillich describes faith in this way: "Faith is the state of being ultimately concerned: the dynamics of faith are the dynamics of man's ultimate concern."[17] This project interprets the dynamics of white supremacist Christianity through a theo-historical discipline, yet the dynamics cannot fully show how faith in white supremacist Christianity is maintained. Faith in this way must be understood as the centered act of the person.[18] It becomes a part of who you are without ever declaring itself.

THE EXISTENTIAL CERTAINTY OF THE WHITE CHRIST

The nondeclarative nature of white supremacist Christianity establishes itself through the production of meaning. The category of space takes shape in the unknowable aspects of the faith. As with other forms of space, adherents to white supremacist Christianity find meaning in the connection of whiteness and Christian values through the construction of a societal system. What makes this form of space different is its transformation from a way of finding meaning in the face of finitude to the elevation of this particular space to the realm of ultimacy. Like Tillich's description of nationalism, white supremacist Christianity becomes central to the identity of white supremacist Christians.[19] The daily strivings of society seek to reinforce the superiority of whiteness through mundane assaults against nonwhites that reinforce the place of whiteness. The "against-each-otherness" nature of white supremacist Christianity necessitates self-abnegation in order to fulfill the greater meaning of communal connection through the identity of whiteness. Everything about one's life that seeks ultimate meaning adheres to the call of whiteness.

Faith as a centered act leads to the aspect of understanding white supremacist Christianity. Tillich applied the demonic in deconstructing the power of Nazism through his radio addresses into Nazi Germany during the last years of World War II.[20] He showed that Nazism had created a system within Germany that provided the German people meaning, in exchange for the destruction of the individual for the benefit of the greater good. In destroying the individual will for a common destiny, Nazism built a society that only found meaning in destruction, and ultimately, its own obliteration. While the young Tillich of the 1920s through the end of World War II applied the demonic to understand the forces that controlled the world in the form of capitalism and totalitarianism, his neglect to discuss race after moving to the United States stunted the cultural significance of the demonic in future works. Certainly, the demonic is a common, yet unnamed, theme in Tillich's radio addresses into Germany, but his use of the demonic as more than a theological theory in his new life in the United States is absent. Tillich taught in New York, Cambridge, and Chicago during the last thirty years of his life, yet he never applied the demonic to the American experience. While Tillich never formally connected the demonic to his adopted country, however, the United States is shaped by everyday iterations of the demonic, particularly the definitive societal structure of white supremacist Christianity. The theo-historical formation of white supremacist Christianity, as constructed in the seventeenth century through the founding of the United States and to its present manifestations, has provided a structure of meaning to the national ethos.

The United States, as a community of beliefs and symbols, is defined through a mythological trajectory with whiteness forming the core of the myth. The United States as a country does not find meaning in the individuality of self, but rather in the universality of the national myth that connects the present to the past through the establishment of symbols as meaning-making markers of Americanness. In these symbols, the community finds meaning in the subversion of self as a determinative aspect of life for the power of the common self.

> The demonic comes to fulfillment in personality, and personality is the most prominent object of the demonic destruction, for personality is the bearer of form in its totality and unconditional character. Therefore, the contradiction of it, the cleavage of personality, is the highest and most destructive contradiction. Therewith, the inner tension of the demonic is disclosed in a new stratum: the personality, the being which has power over itself, is grasped by another power and is thereby divided. This second power is not the law of nature. Demonry is not a relapse to a pre-mental stage of existence. Mind remains minds. In comparison with nature it remains the being which has power over itself. Something else, at the same time, takes possession of it. The other thing contains the vital forces; at the same time, however, it is spiritual and spirit distorting.[21]

Applying the demonic to white supremacist Christianity starts with the history presented in the subsequent chapters. The history of white dominance over and against blacks, indigenous, and others desiring whiteness shows the power of being, as manifested in the character of personality, found in white supremacist Christianity. This points to a larger matrix of operation. This larger matrix is where the demonic lies within the greater American society. White supremacist Christianity has taken "possession," to use Tillich's phrase, of the U.S. ethos.[22]

The reality of white supremacist Christianity is that it cannot function without total obedience. The zealotry of a small percentage, as evidenced in the work of the Ku Klux Klan, cannot maintain the religion of whiteness through extraordinary circumstances; rather, it is the strength of white supremacist Christianity to possess the greater population through its power of meaning. In this way, the mundane iterations manifest the most power. U.S. society reinforces its adherence to white supremacist Christianity, not through slavery and Jim/Jane Crow—which the mythological history of the United States inevitably present as the singular issues of racism—but rather through the everyday insults that reinforce the superiority of white flesh. The everyday wages of whiteness are the arena where meaning is found in the United States through the drive to maintain this system. The soul-distorting nature of white supremacist Christianity is that through the possession of the self with its power of meaning, the individual being is withered through the negation of individual meaning. Tillich describes this as, "demonry has the consequence of destroying the personality through robbing it of being and emptying it of meaning."[23] By removing the individual sense of meaning and replacing it with white supremacist Christianity's sense of meaning, the individual is split because of their inability to be anything beyond the demonic destructive form of their destiny.

The social construction of meaning returns this argument back to Warner Sallman's *Head of Christ*. In the image of Christ presented through the work of Sallman, the meaning of white supremacist Christianity is made manifest. Sallman created *Head of Christ* in 1941. He was inspired by a professor at Moody Bible Institute in Chicago to create a manly looking Jesus.[24] In this painting, Sallman created an image of Jesus that would resonate around the country and give hope and meaning to millions in the grips of World War II and later the Cold War with the Soviet Union. By 1944, Sallman's *Head of Christ* had been reprinted over fourteen million times and purchased by people all over the United States [25] Edward J. Blum and Paul Harvey, in *The Color of Christ: The Son of God and the Saga of Race in America,* describe the effect of the *Head of Christ* in this way:

> Warner Sallman painted what became the most widely reproduced piece of artwork in world history. His *Head of Christ* (1941) adorned living rooms, bedrooms, Sunday Schools, and films. It became a shared resource among Protestants and Catholics, who had fought with each other for so long. Its ubiquity soon inspired countless imitations and parodies, which spoke to but never lessened its power. It was so iconic that to combat card-carrying members of the Communist Party, one American minister wanted every Christian to carry a small print of Sallman's Christ in their wallets. Reproductions of the *Head of Christ* multiplied at an epic rate. Even as white Americans of the civil rights era were compelled to open their schools, neighborhoods, restaurants, borders,

and ballot boxes to non-whites, they held fast to this white vision of Jesus. No matter how many critics denounced its stereotypical white features or his apparent passivity or femininity, this *Head of Christ* became the literal face of Jesus to millions.[26]

The popularity of Sallman's *Head of Christ* in the second half of the American century is undeniable. The popularity of Sallman's *Head of Christ* after World War II is evidenced in the number of prints sold, its use by popular evangelists, and how people viewed it as much more than a painting.[27]

Sallman's Christ became so ubiquitous that Jesus became synonymous with white in the American imaginary. Whether the person was white or nonwhite, the image of Christ in their mind reflected Sallman's work: a white Christ with long flowing hair and a beard, draped in a white robe. Simply put, through the popularity of Sallman's *Head of Christ*, the prime actor in the story of Christianity took on the image of a Euro-Christian. The symbolic became much more than a symbol. *Head of Christ* became the embodiment of white supremacy in the United States. Through the mass reproduction of Sallman's *Head of Christ*, white supremacist Christianity solidified itself in the psyche of the country by replacing individual ideas of Christ with a universal image. It did not matter if the person was white, black, indigenous, or Asian, the symbolic image of salvation became a white man. In this way, the white Christ as symbolized in Sallman's *Head of Christ* possessed the individuality of the Christian faith and superimposed the imagery of a white man as the gateway to salvation.

To take this idea a step further, Anthony Pinn's essay "Putting Jesus in His Place" demonstrates that depicting Jesus as white is more beneficial to whites. This is because whites have come to understand their relationship to Christ through their dominance of the world.[28] White rule has given whites an existential certainty in their closeness to the divine, and yet, trying to reconstruct Christ as black does nothing to diminish this theological feeling of closeness to being Godlike. In fact, to try and change the image of Christ, while seen as important to assuring nonwhite connections to Christ, also reinforces the feeling of superiority within the white mind.[29] The power of the white Christ is its certainty for whites regardless of the claims against it by nonwhites.

In this instance, this involves a blackness created by reaction against a whitened embodiment of *Imago Dei*. Such a move seems to suggest an authentic person can be transfigured through attention to the compromise of time and space offered by the personification of the Christ account. But even this draws one back to the significance of whiteness in that meaning and importance of the blackness of the Christ—the rejection of whiteness as having theological and ontological importance—depends on the perpetual target of whiteness. Hence,

while the blackening of Christ might symbolically and ethically render African
Americans Christ-like, the necessity of whiteness for this development renders
white God-like.[30]

Pinn's point is important to understanding the existential certainty of whiteness as reflected through the white Christ. While it is important to fight the
power of white supremacy, a sleight of hand will not diminish the connection
of whites to their embodied God status. It is this Godlike stature that enabled
the whites of Europe and the United States to dream of owning the world.
Whiteness as a material to be possessed gives unlimited agency to own the
world, even in the face of resistance. In turn, assuring the godliness of whiteness confirms the cultural belief that this is a white man's world.

As Christianity came to the Americas 500 years ago and became the way
in which the explorers understood their encounter with indigenous people
and cultures, so too the American experience came to frame Americanness
through whiteness in the shape of the white Christ. The American experience
makes possible the situation in which the white Christ becomes a symbol of
meaning-making combined with the power of association that holds attach-
ment for white supremacist Christianity within the markers of whiteness as
salvific. Stephen G. Ray, Jr. describes this sense of meaning-making as "the
conditions of sensible use" in his article "Contending for the Cross: Black
Theology and the Ghosts of Modernity." In this article, he explains how
the cross, as a symbol of the Christian faith, is susceptible to use by the Ku
Klux Klan. He explains that with "the term 'conditions of sensible use,' what
I mean to identify is the reality that for a given symbol to exist with some
power in a given context there must be a necessary matrix of ideas and cultural assumptions in which that symbol can be made sensible. Without such
a constellation of ideas a symbol cannot gain the necessary cultural currency
to continue to make sense in that context."[31] The concept of conditions of
sensible use explains the power dynamics that enable the image of the white
Christ to become a symbol with the power of meaning and to continue to
operate in the American context as such. The history of the United States
has constructed a matrix of understanding in which whiteness operates as
the dominant force in the decision-making processes of the historic myth.
Without the myth of the American experience, the symbol of the white Christ
would not be able to subsist in the United States. It is necessary for the symbolization of the white Christ as a marker of white supremacist Christianity
that U.S. history is presented in such a way that continues the mythology of
the American experience.

The soteriology of white flesh as symbolized in the image of the white
Christ brings the American experience to its natural *raison d'être* by creating the systems and matrices of power and meaning that make whiteness

and salvation synonymous. For this reason, the white Christ is not here to save nonwhite bodies because they are beyond salvation in the U.S. psyche. Whiteness is the only marker by which soteriological grounding makes sense in the American experience. For this reason, the American experience is one of white supremacy. It is not a history of equal opportunity; rather, it is a history of white dominance symbolized through a religious matrix of white supremacist Christianity that is epitomized in the all-consuming power of meaning of the white Christ. To rephrase the core argument of this book, the American experience is the worship of the white Christ.

In the second part of the book, the focus will turn to specific historical moments. These moments in history expound the theological arguments of the epistemology of whiteness, the ontology of white supremacy, and the soteriology of white flesh.

NOTES

1. Robert T. Handy, "American Messianic Consciousness: The Concept of the Chosen People and Manifest Destiny," *Review and Expositor* 73, no. 1 (Winter 1976): 49.

2. Rebecca Anne Goetz, *The Baptism of Early Virginia: How Christianity Created Race* (Baltimore: John Hopkins University Press, 2012).

3. Theological destiny developed simultaneously with the pseudoscientific field of ethnology. The study of ethnology transformed theological understandings of race through the study of cultures and peoples.

4. Willie James Jennings, *The Christian Imagination: Theology and the Origins of Race* (New Haven: Yale University Press, 2011), 31.

5. Ibid.

6. Ibid., 32.

7. Ibid., 33–4.

8. The chosenness of whites as the elect is shaped by the particular way in which theology and race interacted with each other in New England. New Englanders provided opportunities for blacks and indigenous people to join the community through involvement in the church, but this did not mean that whites were willing to see themselves as equals. New Englanders considered the possibility that blacks and indigenous people might be redeemed by the Christian gospel, and yet they viewed the racial order as a way to control both groups. In establishing a system of control, the people of New England set up a societal system in which they were ordained by God to construct a racial social order. For more information, see Richard A. Bailey, *Race and Redemption in Puritan New England* (New York: Oxford University Press, 2011).

9. Jennings uses Israel in his construction of supersessionism, yet at this time the idea of Israel was anachronistic. In place of Israel, it would be more appropriate to use "the Jews." Jews had not conceived of themselves as Israel for more

than a millennium by the time Christian supersessionism took shape in theological modernity.

10. Ibid., 36.

11. James W Perkinson, *White Theology: Outing Supremacy in Modernity* (New York: Palgrave MacMillan, 2004). 69.

12. Ibid., 65.

13. Ibid., 21.

14. James C. McKinley Jr., "Texas Conservatives Win Curriculum Change: Texas Conservatives Win Vote on Textbook Standards," *New York Times*, Accessed on March 30, 2016 http://www.nytimes.com/2010/03/13/education/13texas.html?_r=0.

15. Ibid.

16. George Kelsey, *Racism and the Christian Understanding of Man* (New York: Charles Scribner's Sons, 1965), 9.

17. Paul Tillich, *Dynamics of Faith* (New York: Perennial Classics, 2001), 1.

18. Ibid., 4.

19. Paul Tillich, *Theology of Culture*, edited by Robert C. Kimball (New York: Oxford University Press, 1959), 33.

20. Paul Tillich, *Against the Third Reich: Paul Tillich's Wartime Radio Broadcasts in Nazi Germany*, edited Ronald H. Stone and Matthew Lon Weaver (Louisville: Westminster John Knox Press, 1998).

21. Paul Tillich, *The Interpretation of History*, trans. by N.A. Rasetzki and Elsa L. Talmey (New York: Charles Scribner's Sons, 1936), 86–7.

22. Ibid., 87.

23. Ibid., 88.

24. Edward J. Blum and Paul Harvey, *The Color of Christ: The Son of God and the Saga of Race in America* (Chapel Hill: The University of North Carolina Press, 2012), 208.

25. Ibid.

26. Ibid., 12.

27. Ibid.

28. Anthony B. Pinn, "Putting Jesus in His Place," *Humanism: Essays on Race, Religion and Popular Culture* (New York: Bloomsbury Academic, 2015), 77.

29. Ibid.

30. Ibid., 89.

31. Stephen G. Ray, Jr., "Contending for the Cross: Black Theology and the Ghosts of Modernity," *Black Theology* 8, no. 1 (2010): 54.

Part II

THE HISTORICAL FOUNDATIONS OF WHITE SUPREMACY

Chapter 3

The Promised Land

Part One established the parameters for the theological analysis of white supremacy. Each chapter showed how the concepts of epistemology, ontology, and soteriology build on each other in constructing a religion based on the superiority of whiteness. The coming chapters take this theological criticism and apply it to specific historical events. This chapter will build upon the epistemological nature of white supremacy to demonstrate how the British colonists and their American descendants framed Indianness[1] as simultaneously something to be conquered and revered.

Starting with the Pequot War, the epistemology of whiteness exemplifies how the particular way Puritan colonists cosmically understood their place in God's world. This theological ethos informed how the colonists constructed their idea of the New World. Included in this cosmology was the curious presence of the indigenous people. My analysis of the Pequot War is grounded in Mignolo's zero point epistemology. With the "discovery" of how lands west of Europe, the makeup of the world changed for the expanding nations. This meant reimaging the world with Christian Europe at its center. By placing these Christian nations at the center of the world, a new framework of religious epistemology was achieved. The epistemology of whiteness was formed in this recreation of the world. Massachusetts Bay provided the newly arrived Puritans with a place to live out the power of Christianity at the center of the world. The Puritans enacted a theological system in which their God consecrated this new land for their domain.

The idea of discovery made possible the theological rationale that drove Cotton Mather and John Winthrop. Both men viewed their place in the New World as characterized by a special relationship with God. This relationship entitled the Puritans to tame the land, including the indigenous people.[2] The people encountered by the Puritans lacked this special relationship, and thus were insufficient in some manner. The Puritans read this cosmology as signi-fying that they were the people of God while the Pequot were heathens. This worldview harkens directly to a reading of the Jews entering the Promised Land and encountering the Canaanites. Massachusetts became God's Prom-ised Land for God's chosen people. In creating the New World as God's Promised Land, the Puritans initiated a new epistemological framework predicated on their faith as God's superior people. Because they saw them-selves as superior, the Puritan relationship with the Pequot could only entail submission of the ungodly (e.g. heathen) people.

The Pequot War arose out of the desire of the Puritans to expand their con-trol of the Massachusetts Bay area and the Connecticut River. As the settlers expanded their villages, the Puritans entered Pequot communities and killed or took as hostages the women and children.[3] This led to retaliations by the Pequot against English settlements and traders. The relationship between the Pequot and the Puritans based on reprisals culminated in a Puritan leader named John Mason leading soldiers from Massachusetts to annihilate the Pequot.[4] Mason's soldiers targeted the Pequot stronghold on the Mystic River. The men of Massachusetts and Connecticut attacked the fort and killed the Pequot men. Afterwards, the Puritans blocked the entrance to the Pequot fort and set it on fire with the women and children unable to escape the blaze.[5] Puritans like John Mason recalled the massacre at Fort Mystic as the holy act of a godly people. The war with the Pequot sent a clear message to the other indigenous communities on what to expect if these groups would use violence against the Puritans.

The Pequot refusal to abdicate their land and culture was not just an economic issue; it contradicted the very notion of Puritan superiority. Questioning Puritan superiority necessarily meant being beyond the mer-cies of God. Annihilation of the Pequot people was the only way for the Puritans to assert the power of God. The Puritan theological framework made sensible Mather's interpretation of the massacre at Fort Mystic as divinely inspired.

The place of discovery in the mind of the descendants to Puritanism also made sensible the construction of the epistemology of whiteness that informed the United States in the age of Andrew Jackson. The 200 years between the Pequot War and the Indian Removal Act took the idea of dis-covery as a marker of superiority and bestowed it on the American citizenry. What the reader will see between the theology of Cotton Mather and Andrew Jackson is the shift from God making the Puritans the Chosen People and Massachusetts Bay their Promised Land to Jackson's theology, where the American soil always belonged to God's chosen People. No longer did discovery hold special meaning as given to the Puritans in their search for a home. Jacksonian theology was formed by a reinterpretation of discovery as an epistemology of whiteness. This meant that God in the very beginning gave whites dominion over the land of North America.

By understanding God's blessing as eternal, Jacksonian America recast the indigenous people as trespassers on God's land. This theological lens informed the creation, passage, and enforcement of the Indian Removal Act of 1830. The five nations were impinging on God's chosen people claiming the land rightfully given to them. As such, Jacksonian America demanded a divinely mandated *Lebensraum*. The forced removal of Indianness from God's land made right the injustice of ungodly bodies in sacred space.

This line of thinking would continue into the twentieth century with the use of Indian names caricatures as representation for athletic teams. While the physical acts of destruction and removing required by the Puritans and Jackson have ceased, the symbolization of Indianness in such a way provides sacred memorialization of the past.

THE DIVINE WAR AGAINST THE PEQUOT

Starting with the earliest (non-Spanish) colonies in North America, a different approach was taken in relating to the indigenous peoples. On the one hand, Spain's relationship to the colonized resulted in a great debate about the rights of the people in the New World. On the other hand, the white colonizers of Great Britain from the beginning sought cooperation, exploitation, and submission from their indigenous counterparts. As would be expected, this one-sided relationship failed to prosper in both what would become New England and the colony of Virginia. These strained relations would lead to wars between the colonists and the indigenous nations. The most famous of these was King Phillip's War, but there were countless others in an effort to either expel the whites or subdue the indigenous people. These wars often resulted in the white colonizers using overwhelming and disproportionate force against the native population. As Elaine Robinson distills, "Early colonists understood their mission as one of propagating the gospel and Christianizing the 'heathens.'"[6] This is clear by Charles I's decree in the charter for Massachusetts Bay Colony that the conversion of Indians to Christianity must be the primary task of the settlers.[7] This means that from the beginning of the colony, like other colonies in North America, the settlers viewed themselves in a state of superiority in direct opposition to the indigenous peoples who, in their state of being outside of Christian grace, lived lives of uncivilized inadequacy. The conversion of indigenous peoples was only one of several goals the Puritans sought to achieve, of course. The American historical myth strongly emphasizes the drive for religious freedom that the Puritans sought in the "New World," but this was coupled with the prospect of new economic opportunities that manifested themselves in the substantial migration of people from England at the beginning of the 1630s, and it resulted in the founding of several geographically significant cities, like Boston and Cambridge.[8] The growth of the Massachusetts Bay Colony resulted in white settler expansion farther and farther into indigenous lands. This invasion of white settlers quickly moved into the Connecticut River area where they encountered the Pequot nation.[9] This interaction was complicated from the beginning, and within only a few years, the leaders of the Massachusetts Bay Colony sought the elimination of the Pequot people in the first conscious attempt of genocide in modernity.

John Winthrop noted in his writings that early in the encounters of the white settlers and the Pequot people, a treaty was proposed to reach an amicable relationship between the two groups. Alfred Cave notes in *The Pequot War* that while the actual treaty document does not exist, inferences can be made through the writings of John Winthrop.[10] Among the provisions of the treaty were the cession of land by the Pequot to the colony and an agreement that the Pequot would not have to surrender persons who had been connected with the death of English traders before the treaty negotiations.[11] Later, this second provision would be used as a justification for the Puritan colony to attack the Pequot people.[12]

The situation between the Pequot and the colonists never established a lasting peace, and by 1636, there were rumors within the Massachusetts Bay Colony (and settlers along the Connecticut River) that the Pequot people sought the destruction of the colony.[13] While there was no evidence of Pequot hostility after the agreement of the treaty in 1634, the legacy of the murder of the white traders lingered and cast the Pequot as bloodthirsty and violent. The rumors of aggression and possible alliances between local indigenous nations led the leaders of the bay colony to meet with the colony's clergy to determine a course of action. The clergy of the colony said God would bless an attack that called for the murder of all Pequot males and the enslavement of Pequot females.[14] As Elaine Robinson asserts in *Race and Theology*, "when assimilation fails, elimination becomes the alternative."[15] The connection of God with the attacks against the Pequot people also demonstrates how the early settlers of North America came to understand their faith through the ultimacy of space. For God to bless the attack on the Pequot meant that the form of Christianity that the Puritans had adopted took on ultimacy and morphed the Christian God into a god of space, and, as Tillich argues, this god is inherently imperialistic.[16] The initial meeting between the clergy and leaders of the colony resulted in the formation of a military force to quell the Pequot.

Over the next half year, the colony continued to press farther into Pequot territory as well as demand the surrender of those responsible for the death of the white traders, even though the colonists would not reciprocate in kind.

In fact, in his account of English dealings with the Pequot people, Captain John Underhill argues that the colonists never had wronged the Pequot people.[17] These one-way demands by the colonists against the Pequot people are evidence of the "against-each-otherness" of white supremacist Christianity in the American colonies. They foreshadowed the ways in which white society would interact with the indigenous people for the coming centuries. The preferential treatment of white life, even the lowly viewed life of the men killed by the Pequot, was seen as superior to the being of all nonwhites, like the Pequot people. The beliefs of the colonists led to the raising of another army in the fateful spring of 1637.[18] This force embarked to find the main encampments of the Pequot nation, and at the end of their first month of searching, the war party found the Pequot camp at Fort Mystic.

The following passage is from Captain John Mason, the leader of the armed forces sent to destroy the Pequot people:

Capt. Underhill and those with him acted their parts in this tragedy, especially on Mr. Hedge who was the first that entered that gate to which Capt. Underhill led up; the fire was no sooner kindled but the smoke and flames were so violent, that they were constrained to desert the Fort and keep them [the Pequot] in. Thus were they now at their wits end, who not many hours before exalted themselves in their great pride, threatening and resolving the utter ruin and destruction of all the English; exulting and rejoicing with songs and dances; but God was above them, who laughed his enemies, and the enemies of his people to scorn, making them as a fiery oven; thus were the stout hearted spoiled, having slept their last sleep an none of their men could find their hands; thus did the Lord judge among the *heathen*[19], filling the place with dead bodies.[20]

The English account of the battle at Fort Mystic describes a gruesome scene of bloodied and burned bodies trapped by the white settlers and unable to escape the blaze used by the whites to eliminate the Pequot settlement. This battle marks a stark difference between the Spanish approach to indigenous peoples and the predominately English tactic that would create an epistemic lineage of conversion, to attempted extinction, to forced relocation and removal. The history of the Pequot War demonstrates a need by white Christians to establish their own dominion in the "new" world, irrespective of the rights of other beings. Supremacist natural theology established just years after the first English arrived in North America broke open the wages of racism in modernity. The anthropological result of delineating bodies based on an ontic state of good (European or white) versus evil (nonwhite, barbarian, or heathen) destroyed the published mission of the new colonies to convert the indigenous peoples. Had the conversion of the indigenous people ever really been the divine goal of the English and others? Or was it always the creation of a master/slave, Christian/heathen, white/nonwhite theo-political world order based on the anthropological and ontological faith system constructed in the image of whiteness? The creation of white supremacist Christianity enabled the construction of other systems of racial oppression that would take hold throughout the European-dominated world and be justified by its theological and later its philosophical mores.

John Mason's account demonstrates a theological reading of the events. Mason is recounting the destruction of the Pequot people at Fort Mystic as a divinely wrought end. For Mason and other colonists, the Pequot nation became a threat to the ultimacy of their mission in the Massachusetts Bay Colony. It became necessary for the continuation of their divine mission in the wilderness of North America to ensure the destruction of the Pequot people. While Mason would not frame his account in this way, his stating that "God was above them" shows a divine inspiration in the success of the attack. The Pequot War was about what Tillich describes as "special soil."[21] The battle was not simply about the threat the Pequot nation posed to the English settlers. It was about the ultimacy of the English people as Christians against those whom the English god had judged to be heathens in divine space. For this reason, the continued presence of the Pequot people became an assault against the god of white supremacist Christianity as it manifested itself among the people of the Massachusetts Bay Colony.

In *Culture and Redemption: Religion, the Secular, and American Literature*, Tracy Fessenden analyzes how Puritans created a system that made sensible the destruction of the Pequot people. As she argues, the British colonies used a unique way to determine the rights to land. Unlike the French, Spanish, and others, the British did not use the legal system of titles; rather, ownership was defined by their notions of civilization.[22] To claim ownership of particular land meant to build permanent structures, like homes, and to cultivate the land. Neither of these British norms were nonsensical to the indigenous people of Massachusetts. The Puritans used this idea to establish a divine right by demonstrating that the biblical rationale to tame God's creation usurped any rights the Pequot held as previous occupiers of the land.[23] This thinking was further compounded by the Puritans seeing themselves as the Israelites and these "new" lands as marked by God as Canaan. Reading the new colonies as a gift from God was at once a metaphorical and literal reading that justified the clearing of the indigenous people to enable the people of God to prosper.[24] This idea gave the Puritans a cosmic worldview to understand their place in a strange world.

In framing the settling of God's land in cosmic language, the Puritans could turn their focus to the heathenistic image of the indigenous people, particularly the Pequot. This is how the Pequot people drew the ire of the Puritans. The rights of the Puritans to the New Canaan involved the language of spiritual warfare that necessitated the removal of all things Indian from God's land. Fessenden points to Cotton Mather's account to demonstrate that the indigenous people became an obstacle to the ability of God's chosen people to prosper in their new land.[25] This particular viewpoint returns to the concept of space to show that the Puritan theology was one of literal and theological imperialism. In a literal sense, the Puritan people saw the Pequot as a direct threat to their ability to prosper and to reign over God's dominion. Theologically speaking, the figurative and literal presence of the indigenous people was a threat to the power of God to ordain these lands to the Puritan people. Fessenden sees this line of thinking as creating a very real threat to the Puritans based on the Second Commandment.[26]

The dualism of the Puritan world made it virtually impossible to see the indigenous people as possible converts to the faith; rather, their mere presence led to a spatially based identity crisis, as the Puritan drive for purity was impossible with the constant reminder of idolaters in their midst. The indigenous people, particularly the Pequot, became a symbol of the threat to the dominance of white Protestants in God's land. Fessenden even shows how the image of the Indian became a symbol in later generations of colonists of the continued threat posed by others to God's project in America.[27]

CLEARING AMERICA OF HEATHEN BODIES

Two centuries later, a similar debate took place in the then formed United States over the rights and dignity of the indigenous peoples east of the Mississippi River, during a time of substantial white growth and expansion farther west. This type of debate was not new to the United States; what to do with the native populations was a commonplace discussion that often resulted in treaties between the indigenous nations and the white settlers. Often in these treaties, the indigenous peoples relinquished lands in exchange for money and land guarantees. The white peoples used this tactic as a way to continually secure land in the same fashion that Columbus used common European goods to secure precious metals from the Arawak people.[28] The acquisition of land made possible the continual expansion of white settlements and, particularly after the establishment of the United States, the nullification of established treaties for more money, trinkets, and promises in exchange for ever-increasing tracts of indigenous lands in order to secure more living space for the benefit of white individuals.

The bait and switch treaty policies of the North American colonies, and later the United States, are epitomized by the forced removal of the five "civilized" indigenous nations of the American South. By 1830—the year of the inauguration of President Andrew Jackson, the hero of the Battle of

New Orleans and several Indian wars—the state of indigenous peoples east of the Mississippi River was bleak. In the northern United States, many indigenous nations had either moved to escape the ravages of white land grab policies or, with ever-dwindling populations, relocated to smaller properties on reservations.[29] According to Anthony Wallace, the nations of the north, like the Iroquois, posed no significant threat to the economic security of the white nation. The reality in the American South was quite different. The Five Civilized Nations posed a significant economic threat to white America. Unlike in the northern states where the indigenous peoples held relatively small parcels of land in comparison to the white men of the new nation, in the southern states—particularly in the western territories of the Carolinas, Georgia, Florida, Alabama, and Mississippi—the Cherokee, Choctaw, Creek, Chickasaw, and Seminole nations inhabited most of the agricultural land.[30] Indigenous ownership of these lands was an issue for the new nation and its economic stability based on the cultivation of agricultural goods, like cotton. Put simply, the removal of the indigenous peoples was seen as necessary for the economic security of the white nation.

In the presidential administration of Andrew Jackson, these economic concerns found a solution in the decision to justify the forced relocation of the majority of indigenous people east of the Mississippi River to the so-called more hospitable lands in far western territories. Andrew Jackson won the election of 1828 largely due to his support from the southern states that actively desired the relocation of Indians in order to secure their lands to enhance the economic viability of their agricultural economy.[31] Soon after assuming the role of president, Andrew Jackson started to implement the policy of Indian removal that would consume the entirety of his two terms in office.

The fight over who had jurisdiction over the lands in which nations like the Cherokee resided took a turn after the emboldened state of Georgia passed a law declaring that the state claimed jurisdiction over all lands that reside within the border of the state effective in June 1830. This legislation revoked federal policy of independent jurisdiction of all lands inhabited by indigenous nations, and furthermore, it made the Indian nations subject to the laws and statutes of the state of Georgia. As a result of the Georgia legislature's attempt to expand its control, the leaders of the Cherokee nation wrote to the secretary of war seeking support in forcing Georgia to back down from its claim of jurisdiction. The newly appointed secretary of war, John H. Eaton, replied to the Cherokee delegation on April 18, 1829, and clearly stated the position of the Jackson administration.

> To all this, there is a plain and obvious answer, deducible from the known history of the Country. During the War of the Revolution, your nation was the friend and ally of Great Britain; a power which then claimed entire sovereignty,

within the limits of what constituted the thirteen United States. By the declaration of Independence and subsequently the Treaty of 1783, all the rights of sovereignty pertaining to Great Britain, became vested respectively in the original States, of this union, including North Carolina and Georgia, within whose territorial limits, as defined and known, your nation was then situated. If, as this is the case, you have been permitted to abide on your lands from that period to the present, enjoying the right of soil, and privilege to hunt, it is not thence to be inferr[ed], that this was any thing more than a permission growing out of compacts with your nation; nor is it a circumstance whence, now to deny to those states, the exercise of their Sovereignty.[32]

Secretary Eaton further established the new federal policy of Indian removal under the Jackson administration by stating:

In this view of the circumstances connected with your application, it becomes proper to remark that no remedy can be perceived, except that which frequently, heretofore has been submitted for your consideration, a removal beyond the Mississippi, where, alone, can be assured to you protection and peace. It must be obvious to you, and the President has instructed me again to bring it to your candid and serious consideration, that to continue where you are, within the territorial limits of an independent state, can promise you nothing but interruption and disquietude. Beyond the Mississippi your prospects will be different. There you will find no conflicting interests. The United States power and sovereignty, uncontrolled by the high authority of state jurisdiction, and resting on its own energies, your own nation, the soil shall be yours while the trees grow, or the streams run. But situated where you now are he cannot hold to you such language, or consent to beguile you, by inspiring in your bosoms hopes and expectations, which cannot be realized. Justice and friendly feelings cherished towards our red brothers of the forest, demand that in all our intercourse, frankness should be maintained.[33]

Between these two passages from Secretary Eaton's letter to the Cherokee nation, it becomes evident that the mission of the federal government is to force indigenous nations off their land through either coercion or, as history tells through the Trail of Tears, force. A simple reading of Eaton's letter demonstrates a straightforward case of the Jackson administration solidifying Georgia's long-held rights to sovereignty over its own land, but what else could this letter say about federal policy in the middle of the nineteenth century? A critical reading provides evidence of long-held beliefs of white supremacy.

In his letter to the Cherokee nation, Secretary Eaton is emphatically declaring U.S. sovereignty rights over all lands within the charted lines of the United States, whether other people inhabit portions of this land or not. Implicitly, this declaration revokes any claims to sovereignty prior to colonial encounters. This line of thinking, founded upon the civilized versus heathen myth, creates a justification for the white nation of the United States to usurp control over nonwhite lands and self-determined sovereignty. Furthermore, he is arguing a "white is right" line of justification in which all claims to agency by indigenous people are secondary to the needs of whites, who, through their Euro-Christian lineage, take precedence because of their colonial mind-set.

Secretary Eaton's response demonstrates the construction of an identity that drove the decision of the Jackson Administration to push the indigenous nations off their land. While some might believe that Eaton is responding to the Cherokee delegation from a national perspective, his writings show a deeper allegiance that desires the removal of the indigenous peoples from U.S. lands. Eaton points to the dynamism of white thinking in referring to those he is addressing as "red brothers of the forest."[34] Eaton's language points to justification for claiming the land beyond national boundaries. He is claiming a right to the land through the connection of whiteness and civilization. The use of "red brothers of the forest" establishes the Cherokee people as inferior in this dynamic and thereby sets the American government in a place of superiority.

This could only be done through a particular understanding of the place of whites within the makeup of the world. Tillich's conception of space frames the place of whites not as a simple right to specific lands, as Eaton claims. The U.S. desire for the land was founded in a belief of ultimacy as connected to those who judged the indigenous people as inferior. To allow the Cherokee and other nations to remain on the land called into question the legitimacy of the worldview ascribed to Secretary Eaton and his contemporaries. The construction of the particular people who shaped the American nation as anything other than the rightful owners of the land was in direct contradiction to the power of meaning that was driven by the ultimacy of what would later become understood as whiteness. In this situation, Eaton juxtaposes "red brother of the forest" through a null hypothesis that establishes the Americans of the South as the proper owners of the land. This ownership is founded in the divine right of Americanness over and against all other claims to ownership.

The construction of American claims to the land by Eaton received further support by President Jackson. Eight months after Secretary Eaton's response to the Cherokees, President Andrew Jackson addressed the U.S. Congress on the necessities for Indian removal from U.S. territory:

It has long been the policy of Government to introduce among them the arts of civilization in the hope of gradually reclaiming them from a wandering life. This policy has, however, been coupled with another wholly incompatible with its success. Professing a desire to civilize and settle them, we have at the same time lost no opportunity to purchase their lands and thrust them farther into the wilderness. By this means they have not only been kept in a wandering state, but been led to look upon us as unjust and indifferent to their fate. Thus, though lavish in its expenditures upon the subject, Government has constantly defeated its own policy, and the Indians in general, receding farther and farther to the west, have retained their savage habits. A portion, however, of the Southern tribes, having mingled much with the whites and made some progress in the arts of civilized life, have lately attempted to erect an independent government within the limits of Georgia and Alabama. These States, claiming to be the only sovereigns within their territories, extended their laws over the Indians, which induced the latter to call upon the United States for protection . . . Our conduct toward these people is deeply interesting to our national character. Their present condition, contrasted with what they once were, makes a most powerful appeal to our sympathies. Our ancestors found them the uncontrolled possessors of these vast regions. By persuasion and force they have been made to retire from river to river and from mountain to mountain, until some of the tribes have become extinct and others have left but remnants to preserve for a while their once terrible names. Surrounded by the whites with their arts of civilization, which by destroying the resources of the savage doom him to weakness and decay, the fate of the Mohegan, the Narragansett, and the Delaware is fast overtaking the Choctaw, the Cherokee and the Creek. That this fate surely awaits them if they remain within the limits of the States does not admit a doubt. Humanity and national honor demand that every effort should be made to avert so great a calamity.[35]

An initial reading of Jackson's address to the U.S. Congress shows a president deeply concerned for the well-being of the indigenous peoples living in the territories of the United States. He is concerned for the legacy of the American national character, the advancement of civilization among the Indian nations, the prospect of national economic advancement, and the preservation of the Indian peoples. But the hidden message within President Jackson's address to Congress is the legacy of colonial paternalism and the Euro-Christian drive of the civilizing mission.

The mission of civilization and its subsequent colonial paternalism is evident throughout the history of modernity, commencing in the very first encounter in 1492. The creation of modernity with European westward expansion developed a worldview that placed Europeans, and later, the United States, at the center of the world. To put it another way, modernity reconfigured the world like a food chain with Europe and the United States on top with all other peoples fighting not to be on the last rung. This Euro-Christian emphasis creates a theological ecosystem with whites (Western Europeans and English) at the forefront of creation. The force behind this mind-set enabled the accumulation of wealth and power in order to carry out a new white world order.

This New World used the civilizing mission to colonize and reconstruct the periphery of the Euro-Christian world in its own image. Like the theological concept of *imago dei*, the civilizing mission established *imago europam*. "In the image of Europe" meant, as President Jackson stated, "the arts of civilization." In *Race and Theology*, Robinson describes Jackson's "art" as only possible for white persons.[36]

> The "civilizing" process imposed upon the Native Americans included attempts to convert them to Christianity and to educate them in white ways. The Puritans who had survived their first years in America through the aid of Native Americans, soon began to impose laws to control them . . . The infamous quote from Richard H. Pratt attests to the brutality of this Christianizing process: "Kill the Indian in him, and save the man" . . . . Whether Native peoples attempted to assimilate into white culture by force or by choice, it made little difference in the ways they were viewed and treated. White immigrants, self-proclaimed "good Christians," were greedy for land and wealth and created narratives of subhuman peoples unable to conform to civilized norms. Hence, God intended the white man to govern and occupy the land. By 1800, the population of Native Americans in the United States had dwindled to 600,000 and by the end of the nineteenth century their numbers are estimated at a mere 250,000. Not only had they been stripped of their freedom to live and work on lands they had occupied for centuries, but genocide of massive proportions had occurred.[37]

These "arts of civilization" included European reading and writing, an agriculturally based life[38], and the white religion of Christianity. The Euro-Christian understanding of civilization meant the adoption of each of these aspects of life. These ideals of civilization transformed some of the southern indigenous nations, like the Cherokee. The so-called civilized tribes adopted these categories and excelled at assimilation and the accumulation of wealth, but the Indian removal policy of the Jackson administration proved these "civilizing" efforts all for naught. The president's speech, and later the passage of the Indian Removal Act on May 28, 1830, reinforced the supremacy of whiteness in the New World of the United States. While the "civilized" tribes had assimilated to the Euro-Christian culture (members of these nations had significant slave holdings), the realities of white supremacy made it impossible for the people of the Cherokee nations and others to gain full entry into civilized society because, as Jackson's actions intimate, whiteness was the necessary category to be admitted into civilized society:

> "Civilized" or not, Christian or not, they were denied the right to live on their tribal lands which the white Americans wished to possess, arguing that the Native peoples were not "using" or cultivating and developing the land. Adopting white cultural norms and the Christian faith proved insufficient for the First Peoples to enter into the privileges of whiteness.[39]

Whether one is a vagabond or the president of the United States, the key to societal acceptance is the privilege of white skin. The spatialness of white skin created a matrix of divine power and the ultimacy of meaning in the manifestation of white flesh. In symbolization of whiteness is found the mingling of Christianity with white supremacy. President Jackson understood that it was not good enough for the god of space that the indigenous people were practicing the arts of civilization and Christianity. The matrix of Christian, civilized, and white could never be met outside the divine space of the god of white supremacy.

As a result of this worldview, the economic power of some within the Cherokee nation made it necessary to find an avenue to remove them from the southern states, like Georgia, in order to solidify white superiority and the accumulation of white wealth and power. To permit the continuation of Cherokee residence in Georgia was a direct attack against the viability of the Euro-Christian power structure. To maintain power meant the necessity of the continual centering of white supremacy and the removal of any threats to the growth of its power.

The theo-politcal history of white supremacist Christianity is founded in these dichotomous hierarchies of knowledge that constructed modernity with a Euro-Christian focus and not only economically and materially, but religiously. Starting on the cusp of modernity, we can find in history a theological framework of domination commencing with the disembarking of Columbus. With this initial encounter, a triangle of power dynamics created by history, politics, and theology laid the groundwork for the installation of a white supremacist Christianity that can clearly be seen in the interactions of whites and indigenous peoples from the initial conquest, the debates at Vallodolid, the wars of extermination in North America, the Jacksonian policies of Indian removal, and into the twentieth and twenty-first centuries.

THE INDIAN AS POSSESSION

On a cold, snow-covered January night in 1992, the Washington Redskins played in the biggest game of the National Football League season against the Buffalo Bills in Super Bowl XXVI. Inside the Hubert H. Humphrey Metrodome in Minneapolis, Minnesota, the Washington Redskins won their franchise's third Super Bowl. Outside the stadium, a group of 2,000 protesters stood with banners opposing the use of the "Redskins" name and emblem by the Washington professional football team.[40] A few months earlier a similar demonstration had taken place outside the Metrodome protesting the Atlanta Braves of Major League Baseball for their name, emblem, and the use of the "Tomahawk Chop" during the opening game of the World Series between the Atlanta Braves and the Minnesota Twins.[41] In the span of three months, two protests took place outside major U.S. sporting events due to the use of indigenous names, images, and stereotypes by teams participating in their sports most prestigious annual event. Were these outspoken activists a mere aberration within American society? While the media and the respective leagues might want to believe that the events of 1991–2 are unique to their circumstance, the issue of using indigenous names, imagery, and customs as symbols of American athletics, and, more broadly speaking, for consumer goods, is an issue that has not dissipated from the U.S. landscape. There are important legal and civil rights issues involved in using or banning these representations of indigenous people in U.S. culture. The interest here focuses on the symbolization of indigenous nations as commodities of the athletic industry as it manifests on many different levels, including primary, secondary, and higher education as well as professional athletics—in particular, the use of the "Redskins" name and emblem by the professional football team in Washington, D.C.

For over a century, amateur and professional athletic teams have used indigenous people as the basis for their team identity through the use of names, like Indians or Warriors, and team symbols, like Chief Illiniwek (University of Illinois at Urbana-Champaign), Chief Wahoo (Cleveland Indians), and Chief Noc-A-Homa (Milwaukee and later Atlanta Braves). While many teams still use indigenous-inspired names and images, there are notable amateur and professional teams that have changed their name and mascot due to its offensive nature, including Stanford University, University of Massachusetts, Miami University (Ohio), Dartmouth College, and Marquette University.[42]

While many amateur and even some professional teams have changed their names and mascots due to the offensive and often racist connotations they elicit, the issue of using indigenous names and images remains a matter with deep-seated beliefs on both sides of the argument. This reality is no more evident than the controversy surrounding the Washington Redskins. During the second decade of the twenty-first century, this debate over the naming and traditions of the Washington Redskins has received increased media attention, even though indigenous nations and peoples have expressed concern and a desire for these names and symbols to be changed at least since the 1960s.[43]Although groups like the American Indian Movement and the National Association for the Advancement of Colored People have sought the termination of the "Redskins" name and emblem, the league, team owner, and general public have not found the request to be warranted. In September 2014, ESPN released a poll conducted on the use of the Washington Redskins name. In the poll of over 1,000 respondents, 71% believed the Washington Redskins "should not" change their name.[44] At the same time, two-thirds of the respondents believed that the name was not disrespectful.[45] Although 71% seems like overwhelming support for the name, the percentage of support has waned dramatically since a *Washington Post-ABC News* poll in 1992 (the last time the Washington Redskins played in the Super Bowl) when 89% of people believed the team should keep the name.[46]

In response to increased media attention surrounding the use of the "Redskins" name and emblem, Daniel Snyder, the owner and chairman of the Washington Redskins, wrote a letter to the fans of the team. In his letter, Snyder spoke of the pride he has in the team and the appreciation he has for the fans surrounding the Washington, D.C. area and the world. He spoke fondly of being a lifelong fan of the Washington Redskins and the memories of attending games with his father. Snyder said, "the tradition—the song, the cheer—it mattered so much to me as a child, and I know it matters to every other Redskins fan in the D.C. area and across the nation." Snyder continued, "Our past isn't just where we come from—it's who we are."[47] Snyder is correct that memories are important and that our history defines who we are today. This is part of the task of this project. To better understand our past as the United States in order to further comprehend who "we" are as a nation now and in the future. But what history is the United States telling? More importantly, what history is not being told, particularly when discussing the traditions and practices associated with the Washington Redskins?

In his letter to the fans, Snyder refers to his times attending Washington Redskins games as a child with his father and participating in the singing and cheers with the rest of the fans at the game. What song and cheers is Snyder referring to? The Washington Redskins have a tradition of singing "Hail to the Redskins" throughout the games played in Washington, D.C. "Hail to the Redskins" was written in 1938. Barnee Breeskin wrote the tune for the song, and he made it reminiscent of "Jesus Loves Me."[48] The fight song included lines like "Fight for old Dixie" and "Scalp'em, swamp'em."[49] The lyrics would subsequently be changed in the 1960s, yet the line "Braves on the Warpath" remained from the original version. The history of "Hail to the Redskins" is not surprisingly based on the early history of the team. Before the creation of the Dallas Cowboys, the Washington Redskins were the only professional football team in the southern states.[50] They held a monopoly within the professional football leagues on their connection to the south.[51]

Returning to Snyder's statement, the notion that "our past isn't just where we come from—it's who we are" is made more complicated by knowing some of the history of the team. The fact is, the Washington Redskins have a history of using racist connotations, imagery, and practices that call into question the continued use of the name and images. The contemporary use of the name "Redskins" and the imagery is not an isolated issue. It is a continuation of abuse and misuse that can be traced back to the first accounts of the indigenous peoples of North America by the British during the seventeenth century. From the initial colonies, the interaction of the British in North America, and the U.S. policy of Indian removal during the age of Manifest Destiny through to the present era, the lives of Indians and their representations have been sites of exploitation by Euro-Americans for centuries.

The resolve to continue with the use of the Redskins name by Snyder demonstrates a particular force of righteous indignation in the face of growing pressure to change the name. Paul Tillich addressed this form of indignation in his radio message entitled "Collective Guilt." This particular address was delivered within weeks of Operation Gomorrah, carried out by the British Air Force, in which the city of Hamburg was fire bombed in the last week of July 1943. When the bombing finished, the German people were shocked by the destruction, and this is what Tillich focused on in his radio broadcast.

In this address, Tillich argues that the people of Germany must accept their guilt for what has happened in Europe and for what is happening to their country—not because they are completely responsible for what was happening, because all nations involved are responsible for the carnage of the war, but because they are particularly responsible for the rise of Nazism in Germany. The German people did not recognize the demonry of Nazism and instead accepted Nazism as a way to return to greatness, and all it did was destroy the county more than could have ever been imagined after World War I.[52] In this way, Tillich argues that Germany must accept its guilt, along with the defeat that is inevitable, and help to rid the world of the Nazi threat that will destroy the country. To accept this guilt will enable the country to remove the shackles of National Socialism and be reborn. Without accepting this guilt, the whole country of Germany becomes responsible for the actions of National Socialism, including the death of tens of millions, the death and persecution of people in camps and the countryside of Eastern Europe, and the destruction of the German nation.[53] Ultimately, the people of Germany must accept their guilt and work to help the world move forward, to help Germany move forward.

The persistence in using the Redskins moniker has parallels to the denial confronted in Tillich's address. While the stakes were higher for the people of Germany than for those who support the continued use of the racialized team name, the demonic power of white supremacist Christianity is just as real as that of Nazism in the waning years of the war. The continued use of the name points to and even strengthens the claims of white superiority while simultaneously purporting to "honor" the history of indigenous people. This belief can only be possible through the observance of a demonic divine. The demonic blinds its followers to the destructive nature of the Redskins name and image by making followers take pride in the legacy of the name. While the name is an eternal reminder of the genocide and continued second-class status of indigenous people in the United States, the foggy lenses of the demonic enable the followers of the religion of whiteness to see a history that is drastically different from the historical record. In accepting that the Redskins name and image should be changed, the adherents to whiteness could break the cycle of demonry. Other countries have taken this step. This step could lead to the destabilization of the whole white supremacist faith system in the United States.

The use of the "Scalp'em, swamp'em" and "Braves on the warpath" connects back to the history of early colonists wars, particularly with the Pequot. This language describes the eternal heathenness of indigenous people that were seen as outside God's care and a threat to the Christian way of life. This song is the continuation of a 300-year-old mythos that puts the Indian outside the boundaries of civilized people. One must be able to connect the history of how the United States constructed the Indian within its psyche to understand the religiosity of the Redskin name and emblem. Vincent L. Wimbush's idea of scripturalization helps make sense of how Snyder and others see the Redskins' name and emblem.

> It (scripturalization) refers to more than a text, although clearly the "text" that was the Bible and those texts one might call parascriptural were certainly important sites of intense focus. But the term more broadly refers to the ideology and power dynamics and social and cultural practices built around texts. It refers to the uses of texts, textuality, and literacy as a means of constructing and maintaining society, as a legitimation of authority and power. It becomes shorthand for a type of structure and arrangement of power relations and communications of society, the ultimate politics of language. It is nothing less than magic, a powerful and compelling construction of make believe.[54]

For this instance, the reader must remember the almost four centuries of European interaction with the people of the Americas. This history is what makes sensible a caricature of an indigenous person with clay-red skin and feathers in his hair as the symbol of a sports team.

Turning back to the Spanish debates around the status of those the colonizers called "heathens" begins this trajectory. Discerning the place of the heathen comes from a debate over the theological interpretation of scripture. The way in which the power structures read the Bible onto society would construct the very foundations of who was protected and who was not. For Spain, this meant the forming of colonies in North and South America in which conversion and civilization were the end result of indigenous servitude. While this was not necessarily the reality, the formal power emanating from Spanish crown deemed this the ultimate aim.

The Puritans a century later took the heathen construct to mean a very different reality in Massachusetts and Connecticut. From the outset, the Puritan scriptural understanding constructed the heathen as the outside enemy. The Pequot were not just strangers; they were an assault on God's promised people and their new land. As such, the power of God's promise stood as a guarantee to the Puritan people as sanctuary from the threat of outside forces, for example the Pequot. The making of the Pequot as the ungodly stranger also made it necessary to destroy the Pequot people who did not submit to the superior place of God's people. The theological framing is made clear in Mason's account of the burning of Fort Mystic by using the language of pleasing God.

The theology of blessedness given to the Puritans as opposed to the Pequot enabled the beginning of a national identity for the new inhabitants.

> The same mentalité or "reading" that made the people believe (in) the "reality" of the "nation" also made them, as citizens of the nation, believe (in) the "reality" of "scriptures"—of and for the nation. The one was impossible without the other. The one facilitated belief in the other. Without the make-believe facilitated by "scriptures"—among other factors and considerations, to be sure—the "nation" was only a collection of people sharing space and time. Without the make-believe facilitated by the "nation," the "scriptures" called the "Bible" were only collections of texts, important perhaps to some, but not powerful in absolute terms. In this situation one type of magic created and enhanced the other.[55]

For the Puritans, their faith led them to North America, but the encounter with indigenous people meant the scriptures that brought them together to traverse the ocean also had to be comprehended in a way that differentiated them from the encountered peoples. Wimbush's concept of magic illumines the religiosity of the movement in Puritan North America. The Bible had brought the people together, but in the face of foreign diversity, a new connection had to be made to solidify the meaning of the Puritans on this new shore. This magical creation is shown in the accounts of the Pequot War.

While the Puritans understood their place as God's chosen people in a new Promised Land, Andrew Jackson built upon this theological power relation as God's chosen nation. In arguing for the removal of the Five Civilized Nations, Jackson took the Puritan idea of the Promised Land and focused on the wandering native. Their "savage habits" demonstrated that indigenous people should not be surrounded by civilized white persons. Jackson created an argument that the five nations must be moved to ensure the sanctity of the young nation and simultaneously affirmed the honor of the American nation by also ensuring that indigenous people remained the stranger in need of removal. Wimbush would see this construction of two eternally distinct people as part of the creation of nationalization.

Within the sphere of the "unbounded influence" that is experienced as scripturalization as nationalization, it is a matter of importance who has facility and authority to read and interpret what "God" "says" in scriptures. All will always agree that knowing what "God"—that English abbreviation for the ultimate—wants or requires is important. All agree that wills to reveal what God wants and requires; this is simply another way of indicating what is imperative for the society as a whole. The challenge is to find out what was the shape and secret of the revelation. So the protocol or method by which such revelation can be divined is most important.[56]

Applying Wimbush's nationalization to Jackson's comments on removing indigenous people uncovers that his understanding of nation means the removal of the stranger. While Puritans understood the Pequot as an existential threat to their place as god's people, Jacksonian America had evolved. Now, the indigenous stranger threatened the preservation of God's chosen nation. The stranger was the reminder of not fulfilling God's promise. While Jackson's address to Congress focused on protecting the indigenous people by making them move west of the Mississippi River, he was actually ensuring the fulfillment of the promise first sought in Massachusetts. The "magic," as Wimbush describes it, is the construction of a society ordained by a God that only members of the in-group could comprehend. The reality of the civilized nations is that no matter their ability to "read" the scripture of the white religion, they will always be the eternal stranger. This is the crux of the religion of white supremacy as "scripturalized" on American society. The "Indian" is the stranger. No matter the Indian's ability to acquire the attributes of civilized, America's first requirement is to be white, which is inherently to not be the stranger, to not be the heathen.

Wimbush's scripturalization concept renders sensible the growth of white supremacy from the Puritans to Andrew Jackson and finally to the "Indian" as sports spectacle. The development of the indigenous as the eternal stranger means that the Indian becomes the symbol of the inverse of God's chosenness as depicted in whiteness.[57] As such, by the time the United States moves from Jacksonian America to the present situation, the symbolization of the Redskin has become a memorialization of the eternal stranger. The Redskin as memorial is the perpetual reminder of the white Christian conquering of the lands that represent the United States. The Redskin as a symbol of this conquering points back to the massacre at Fort Mystic that was ordained by the God of the Puritans.[58] The Redskin represents the taming of America by the removal of the savage to make room for the civilized (white) people to move further west. The use of the Redskin is a subtle way for whites to assure themselves of their chosenness by God to rule these lands.

The Redskin has become a part of the very fabric of the scripturalization of whiteness. To many, it seems to be an innocuous symbol of a football team, but it holds the power—or as Wimbush states, "magic"—of white dominance of societal structures.[59] Returning to Snyder's letter, he argues that through the tradition of the Redskin name the team is honoring indigenous people. While he might truly believe that the team is honoring indigenous people, the very presence of the Indian face on the team helmet represents a different history. The Redskin is the continuation of the casting out of indigenous people that started with the Puritans. The Redskin is a memorial of this history. To whites, the Redskin is a part of the cultural scripture of the United States. This reality makes it nonsensical to supporters of the Redskin symbol to see it as anything but honoring native people.

As with the construction of the barbarian and the heathen narratives, the "Redskins" moniker and imagery point to a white society that is claiming superiority and power over indigenous peoples by appropriating their very being (through stereotypes or not) for the pleasure of non-Indian spectators. As the colonizing powers declared the indigenous nations inferior to their Christianity and President Jackson saw them as a hindrance to the spread of the white race, the United States currently instills its superiority by using caricatures of indigenous people and nicknames much in the same way that medieval and early modern Christians in Europe employed ones of Jews.[60] The Christian foundation of this practice connects the current use of indigenous caricatures to a particular theological understanding of native people as inferior to the white Christian power dynamic in the United States.

As Daniel Morley Johnson explains, the power of naming is crucial to this power dynamic.

> We might understand this aspect of the European American obsession with naming, a symbolic act that requires the self-appointed authority to name (both people and places) and, in this case, the power to ridicule and create an Other that is ridiculed in schools and in the professional sports industry. European colonizers have proclaimed for themselves the right to name (and hence claim) most of the world and the world's peoples—so the team nicknames "Redskins" and "Chiefs" share a genealogy with those nations and people who were renamed in the minds of invading Europeans.[61]

As with the foundations for European and later U.S. claims to indigenous lands based on the civilized Christian and savage heathen binary, so too, schools and sports teams find it to be their right to exploit and own the legacy of native persons through naming and the appropriation of images. These names and images are symbols of the white supremacist Christian because they point to the religious victory of Christians over the heathens for the glorification of the god of white supremacy in the U.S. Symbols—like Redskins, Chiefs, Braves, and Indians among many others—are a religious totem of the Christian victory in the Americas.

The continued use of the Redskins team name by Washington points to an important dialectic within American white supremacy. Philip Deloria describes this dualism as "playing Indian." In his book, *Playing Indian*, Deloria argues that throughout the history of the United States (starting with the Boston Tea Party to the present), the concept of Indian and the national identity have developed together.[62] The same interplay is seen in the history of the Washington Redskins. On one hand, you have the dualism of Washington, D.C. being the epicenter of American identity as the seat of national power. On the other hand, there is a football team named after a host of peoples and nations that psychologically do not exist anymore in the eyes of the white nation because of the white nation.

Of the many dualisms constructed by Deloria, the most important to this book is the noble savage. After close to 250 years of Indian play, the Redskins are now one of the more recognized ways in which Indianness remains a part American culture.[63] In the case of the Washington Redskins, there is power found in the dualism of the noble savage. There are fans of the team who employ the noble aspect of Indian play every game day as the team and fans come together through the reaffirmation of their common identity. This is done through various rituals of donning Indian garb that ranges from clothing with the name and emblem on it to appropriated Indianness found in headdresses or other essentialized pieces of clothing. The team says it is honoring the place of Indians in America through dress and ritualized actions.[64] In providing a sense of community, the football team on every Sunday provides a temporal and spatial break for its participants from the angst of modern life. Speaking of what he terms "hobbyists" who attend weekend powwows, Deloria says, "They played Indian in order to address longings for meaning and identity that arose from the anxieties of their time." I would argue the Redskins' football games could represent a more casual form of the weekend powwow. The games give rejuvenating power while at the same time enabling the spectators to not have to forfeit the power of white space.

While the team insists on only recognizing the noble piece of the dialectic, the other side is the savage Indian constantly played out in the image of conquered people driven from white space. "At the very same time that it was suggesting Indian's essential place in the national psyche, playing Indian evoked actual Indian people and suggested a history of conquest, resistance, and eventual dependency."[65] The act of playing Indian for the team is a double take of white supremacy. While finding meaning and community through the rituals of a football game, the team and supporters are simultaneously taking and "honoring" the Indian past in American history. It is important to highlight that the team is not pointing to the life of Indians today or even that exist. The team is honoring the freedom the noble Indian of the past represents. And yet, the team wants to forget how present American society got to the historical moment where the only Indian remembered is the dead one.

The double take of white supremacy is in acting out the idealized form of the noble Indian of the past, while also forgetting how white society systematically fought for the destruction of the savage Indian. The noble Indian of the past is the same as the one that white ancestors called the savage Indian. Curiously, white supremacy on both accounts acts as if Indianness is an object to possess. This is the religion of white supremacy in action. The Washington Redskins are a double take acted out in white space for the white God. The noble Indian of the past is idealized for his place outside modern problems, yet the place of living Indians is outside white consciousness. On the other hand, the savage Indian is a reminder of the power of the white God's ability to ensure the preservation of white space.

By depicting indigenous people as objects of spectacle as a part of a sporting event, a nonverbal history of white dominance is continued that started with the very verbal and violent invasion of Christians from Europe into the Americas. The theological drive to define the indigenous nations in terms of cosmic understandings of good and evil, civilized and uncivilized, and Christian and unchristian has had an indelible affect on the United States. In constructing the binary, Europeans, and later Americans, used their theological understanding of the world to construct a system in which Christianity ensured its dominance throughout the Americas, in particular the United States, by asserting and continually reasserting a theological supremacy in order to physically, psychologically, and spiritually annihilate the indigenous people of the Western Hemisphere. The drive to subdue the people of the Americas through a theology of white supremacist Christianity could not and would not be the conclusion of the Euro-American drive for dominance.

CONCLUSION

This chapter took the idea of the epistemology of whiteness and applied it to the relationship of the white God with the indigenous people encountered in what would become the United States. The chapter began by showing how the Puritan settlers used a cosmic understanding of space to justify the forced removal of the Pequot people from the new colony. This hyperviolent act that included the massacre at Fort Mystic established the context in which the religion of white supremacy would provide ultimacy to its followers in relationship with all other peoples who operated at the fringes of white space.

This took a step further during the Jacksonian era with the removal of the Five Civilized Nations from the American southeast to ensure uncontested land for whites as they desired to expand the richness of agricultural trade in the United States. The rationale for moving the five nations hinged upon the belief in the ultimacy of white supremacy that gave white persons a divine right to the land occupied by Indian bodies. Jackson seized upon this aggression toward Indian interlopers by forcibly removing Indian bodies from white space in an American form of *Lebensraum*.

The final piece of the chapter showed how contemporary forms of white supremacy work to ensure the power of white supremacy by ritualized depiction of Indianness in American culture. This was done through looking at the Washington Redskins as an example of the white God possessing Indianness.[66] This made the place of the Indian within American culture an act ritualization and a constant reminder of the conquest of the heathen in the midst of white space.

This chapter takes the relationship of whites and indigenous people in the United States to show how a dialectic of superiority developed over three centuries. The Pequot War, Indian removal, and the existence of the Washington Redskins demonstrate how the progression of the epistemology of whiteness transformed over the centuries. This scripturalized knowing lays the foundation for the religion of white supremacy to reveal the ontological power of the faith. The next chapter will build on the knowledge of eternal difference to show how whites furthered their society based on an embodied superiority of difference.

NOTES

1. In reference to Indianness, I am not referring to the people of India as the term is commonly understood.

2. Alfred Cave, *The Pequot War* (Amherst: The University of Massachusetts Press, 1996), 170 and Cave, 35.

3. Roxanne Dunbar-Ortiz, *An Indigenous Peoples' History of the United States* (Boston: Bean Press, 2015),

4. Ibid.

5. Ibid.

6. Elaine A. Robinson, *Race and Theology* (Nashville: Abingdon Press, 2012), 62.

7. Angie Debo, *A History of the Indians of the United States* (Norman: University of Oklahoma Press, 1984), 47.

8. Ibid., 46.

9. Ibid., 47.

10. Alfred Cave, *The Pequot War* (Amherst, MA: University of Massachusetts Press, 1996), 71.

11. Ibid., 70–2.

12. John Mason, *Major Mason's Brief History of the Pequot War* (Boston: S. Kneeland & T. Green in Queen-Street, 1736), 17.

13. Cave, *The Pequot War*, 99.

14. Ibid., 109.

15. Robinson, *Race and Theology*, 62.

16. Paul Tillich, *Theology of Culture*, edited by Robert C. Kimball (New York: Oxford University Press, 1959), 32–33.

17. John Underhill, *Newes From America; or, A New and Experimental Discoverie of New England* (London: F.D., 1638), 11.

18. Cave, *The Pequot War*,144.

19. Emphasis added by the author.

20. John Mason,. *Major Mason's Brief History of the Pequot War* (Boston: S. Kneeland & T. Green in Queen-Street, 1736), 30.

21. Tillich, *Theology of Culture*, 32.

22. Tracy Fessenden, *Culture and Redemption: Religion, the Secular, and American Literature* (Princeton: Princeton University Press, 2007), 19.

23. Ibid., 21.

24. Ibid., 22.

25. Ibid., 24.

26. Ibid., 23.

27. Ibid., 38.

28. Christopher Coiumbus, *The Four Voyages of Christopher Columbus* ed. and trans. by J.M. Cohen (New York: Penguin Books, 1969), 17–8.

29. Anthony F.C. Wallace, *The Long, Bitter Trail: Andrew Jackson and the Indians* (New York: Hill and Wang, 1997), 30.

30. Ibid.

31. Robert V. Remmi, *Andrew Jackson and His Indian Wars* (New York: Viking, 2001), 225.

32. Francis Paul Prucha, ed., *Documents of United States Indian Policy* (Lincoln: University of Nebraska Press, 1990), 45.

33. Ibid.

34. Prucha, ed. *Documents of United States Indian Policy*, 45.

35. Ibid., 47–8.

36. Ibid., 47.

37. Robinson, *Race and Theology*, 63.

38. President Jackson's understanding of agricultural life was different from John Locke's in *Second Treatise of Government*. Locke's exposition "On Property" enumerates property as the use of enough land and resources to enable a person and their dependents to survive. What Jackson was arguing was that the civilized art of agriculture is the accumulation of capital by ever-growing consumption of land in order to gain more wealth in the form of money. The land in question is particularly important to the accumulation of wealth because the slave economy is only sustainable if slaveholders can continuously expand their landed property for their human property to work.

39. Robinson, *Race and Theology*, 63.

40. Ken Denlinger, "Protest of 'Redskins' Draws 2,000 at Stadium," *Washington Post*, January 27, 1992.

41. Marc Topkin, "Native Americans Protest Braves Outside Metrodome Series: World Series Notebook," *St. Petersburg Times*, October 20, 1991.

42. Joseph J. Hemmer, Jr., "Exploitation of American Indian Symbols: First Amendment Analysis," *American Indian Quarterly* 32, no. 2 (Winter 2008): 121.

43. Sudie Hofmann, "The Elimination of Indigenous Mascots, Logos, and Nicknames: Organizing on College Campuses," *American Indian Quarterly* 29, nos. 1&2 (Winter & Spring 2005): 156–8.

44. "New Poll Says Large Majority of Americans Believe Redskins Should Not Change Name," *Washington Post*, September 2, 2014.

45. It is interesting to note the 3% that found the "Redskins" name to be disrespectful, and yet also believed the name "should not" be changed to something more respectful.

46. "New Poll," *Washington*, Sep. 2, 2014.

47. "Letter From Washington Redskins Owner Dan Snyder to Fans," *Washington Post*, October 9, 2013.

48. Locke Peterseim, "Not Just Whistling Dixie in D.C.,"*ESPN*, accessed February 22, 2015, http://espn.go.com/page2/wash/s/closer/020315.html.

49. Ibid.

50. In addition to this, the Washington Redskins were the last professional football team to integrate and only did so by succumbing to public pressure.

51. Ibid.

52. Tillich, *Paul Tillich's*: *Theologian of the Boundaries*, edited by Mark Kline Taylor (San Francisco: Collins Publishers, 1987), 179.

53. Ibid., 181.

54. Vincent L. Wimbush, *White Men's Magic: Scripturalization as Slavery* (New York: Oxford University Press, 2012), 87.

55. Ibid., 113–4.

56. Ibid., 125.

57. Ibid, 155.

58. Mason, *Major Mason's Brief History of the Pequot War*, 30.

59. Wimbush, *White Men's Magic*, 87.

60. For more information on the history of Christian anti-Semitism, see James Carroll, *Constantine's Sword: The Church and the Jews* (New York: Mariner Books, 2002).

61. Daniel Morley Johnson, "From the Tomahawk Chop to the Road Block: Discourses of Savagism in Whitestream Media," *American Indian Quarterly* 35, no. 1 (Winter 2011): 105–6.

62. Philip J. Deloria, *Playing Indian* (New Haven: Yale University Press, 1998), 2.

63. There are other representations that are prominent in American culture, as represented by other sports teams, Disney movies, and Halloween costumes, to name a few.

64. Deloria. *Playing Indian*, 174.

65. Ibid., 186.

Chapter 4

The Ritual of Sacrifice

As the epistemology of whiteness solidified itself in the American psyche, it became necessary to ensure that the community of God's people stayed intact. To this end, God's people began to take the knowledge of being superior and embody its meaning. This chapter shows how the knowledge of superiority became a way of being that is necessary for the preservation of the ideology of white supremacy. The idea of sacrifice is pivotal in making the religion of white supremacy what it is. The use of sacrifice elucidated in this chapter is one of separation. The sacrifice of separation is about ensuring the purity of whiteness. Through analysis of two episodes which resulted in the deaths of black, the chapter elucidates the fundamental differences between the successful sacrifice of an individual through lynching as opposed to an instance where a lynching event is denied. Yet, the sacrifice of separation is not limited to realities of physical death. The need to preserve whiteness has also meant the physical casting out of black bodies. Each historical piece defines a different element of this separation.

In this chapter, I continue to construct the theo-historical account of this demonic form of Christianity that was described in the previous chapter. In addition, I turn my focus to the legacy of white supremacist Christianity's development as a social construct as it pertains to the bloody and oppressive treatment of African-Americans from the colonial establishment of slavery through the ghettoization of U.S. cities and the government-instituted housing apartheid system of recent decades. The historical moments treated in this chapter are the Tulsa Race Riot, a lynching in Marion, Indiana, and the construction of the Eight Mile–Wyoming (E-W) wall in Detroit, Michigan. As with the previous chapter, I start by creating a historical account as a primary lens and then turn to how other historical realities, like chattel slavery, lynching, and segregationist housing policies weave together to create a dynamic account of systematic racial oppression and the creation of a system, through theological, philosophical, and political means, that created a society for whites and for the benefit of whites at the cost of others.

THE BLACK TRANSGRESSION OF WHITE SPACE

On May 31, 1921, a young man named Dick Rowland entered an elevator in Tulsa, Oklahoma. Years earlier this young man had dropped out of high school to pursue a career in shoe shining in this relatively wealthy town in the former Indian Territory. On the elevator with him was a seventeen-year-old woman who operated the elevator. As Mr. Rowland exited the elevator, he stumbled and bumped into the young woman. This historical account in itself is not remarkable or even out of the everyday experience of human life, but this chance encounter ended very differently in the town of Tulsa. Within 48 hours of this fateful encounter, Dick Rowland was in jail for the accused rape of Sarah Page,[1] looting and fire had decimated at least ten square blocks,[2] and at least thirty-two people were dead.[3] What about this event could have caused this destruction? Surely, running into someone is not a crime, but in this case a criminal offense had apparently been committed. Out of context, this is a shocking reality, but Mr. Rowland was a black man who had stumbled into a seventeen-year-old white woman in early twentieth-century Oklahoma. The events prior to the riot, including the failed attempt to lynch Rowland, are not a primary concern to this argument. In fact, in the weeks after the Tulsa Race Riot or war, as some have called it, Dick Rowland was released from jail and consensus held that the accused rape did not take place. The history of the race riot that occurred in the hours after the events in the elevator between Mr. Rowland and Ms. Page are definitive in understanding the existential reality of blacks in the United States and the history of white supremacist Christianity and its formation.

In the hours after the encounter between Dick Rowland and Sarah Page, the city police force tried to ascertain the whereabouts of Rowland. Beyond the course of normally searching for a suspect in a criminal offense, the police needed to find Rowland, a young black man, to prevent what had happened to many others like him in the postbellum United States, particularly in the post-Reconstruction south. As Chris Messer argues in "The Tulsa Race Riot of 1921: Toward an Integrative Theory of Collective Violence," Dick Rowland was at a racial impasse between being a young man who stumbled into a young woman and a black body of spectacle.[4] In fact, in the fourteen years prior to the Tulsa Race Riot, at least twenty-six African-Americans were lynched in Oklahoma, and more recently, in 1920, a white mob had lynched a black man on the outskirts of Tulsa. This existential reality led the black community of Tulsa to fear the perceived inevitable fate of Rowland as another name and body accounted for in the legacy of lynching. To compound these fears, the *Tulsa Tribune* in its afternoon edition printed a front page story titled, "Nab Negro for Attacking Girl in Elevator," detailing the event that had taken place at the Drexel Building and stated that Rowland had been arrested attempting to assault a "white" girl.[5] The newspaper used the idea of sacred white womanhood to incite the Tulsa community to realize the attack on white space. Publishing an article detailing a supposed sexual encounter between a black man and a white woman would necessitate action by the white community to protect the fidelity of whiteness.[6] The mayor and the chief of police, who both stated that Dick Rowland had not molested Sarah Page, directly contradicted this article by the *Tulsa Tribune*,[7] but this did not stop the white residents of Tulsa from believing the report in the *Tulsa Tribune*. In the days after the riot, the newspaper would admit to deceiving the public. Within an hour of the evening edition of the newspaper being published, there was talk in Tulsa of apprehending Rowland in order to lynch him.[8] With the talk of a possible lynching, city officials agreed it was prudent to quietly move Rowland from the city jail to the county jail on the third floor of the county courthouse for added security against the possibility of a lynch mob attempting to overtake the jail, as often happened in other accounts of lynchings.[9]

It did not take long for the white citizens of Tulsa to know Rowland had been moved to the county jail, and a crowd started to form around the courthouse building. By 7:30 P.M., it was estimated that over 300 presumably white protesters had surrounded the courthouse and refused to disperse when ordered to do so by the chief of police and the county sheriff.[10] For the next two hours the crowd at the courthouse continued to grow when a group of African-Americans, no more than thirty, approached the courthouse. Some of the members of both groups were armed, and the police convinced the black group to disperse in order to avoid a violent conflict, while the white crowd again refused to cooperate with law enforcement. A short time later, as the white crowd surpassed 2,000, an estimated group of seventy-five African-Americans approached the courthouse again with intent of protecting Rowland from a possible lynching.[11] As members of the black group traversed the white crowd, an unidentified white person tried to disarm one of the black men, resulting in the discharge of a firearm. For roughly the next twelve hours, the city was an active war zone.

The immediate altercation at the courthouse involved an indeterminate number of perpetrators, but there are reports that the police took part in shooting at black persons as they ran from the courthouse. The initial altercation resulted in two fatalities, both of them African-American men.[12] As the African-American group retreated from the courthouse, the police deputized between 250 and 500 white men to quell the black population.[13] This new deputized force used their government-sanctioned powers to loot local stores for weapons, among other everyday necessities, and then proceeded to organize an attack on the black neighborhood of Greenwood. By 10 P.M., the police, with its substantially inflated numbers and arms, descended on Greenwood, or as some whites called it, "Little Africa."[14] Within an hour, the police established a military-style perimeter between Greenwood and the rest of Tulsa, and the police force of regular citizens and trained officers began to arrest black residents. At the same time that white citizens started arresting blacks, both sides started to engage each other with firearms and other weapons, which would later include the reported use of airplanes using incendiaries on the structures in Greenwood.

This fighting continued well into the night, but by dawn the white force had become a vigilante force seeking the destruction of anything in Greenwood, including its residents. In the morning hours of June 1, the white mob began to pillage black businesses and houses and systematically torch the buildings.[15] By this time, the fighting between the white mob that was estimated at 20,000–25,000 and the black residents came to bloody end as the black residents began to flee Tulsa.

As whites took control of Greenwood, it became clear that anything associated with black life was disposable. There are reports of black bodies being dragged through the streets by cars filled with armed white men at the helm[16] and blacks being executed by the vigilante police while trying to surrender,[17] and those who were not killed or driven away were apprehended and marched through the streets of Tulsa to be interned at a makeshift detention center at the city convention center.[18] In these descriptions, one is reminded more of the clearing of Jewish ghettos by Nazis than the untold fringes of U.S. history.[19]

The aftermath of the riot is as instructive as the actual events and destruction that took place that evening. As the embers cooled and the National Guard took control of the city, the damage from the night's events became shockingly apparent. Thirty-two blocks of Greenwood were destroyed, including the business district.[20] Blacks fled or were killed or interned, and if any of those who had fled returned, they were interned as well. The neighborhood lost everything, while the whites of Tulsa blamed the blacks for inciting a riot. "The first step toward prosecution of alleged leaders of the race riot and subsequent burning of the Negro district here last week with a cost of thirty-two lives, was taken today with the filing of charges against K.B. Stratford, Negro, and former hotel proprietor, and three other negroes, none of whom is in custody. They are charged with rioting." The same article went on to state "orders have been issued by the police department that beginning Wed. [*sic*] morning [July 8, 1921] all negroes found on the streets without identification cards will be arrested and placed in a detention center."[21] The article demonstrates the position of the city in placing culpability for the riot squarely on its black population. K.B. Stratford, like many other black professionals, lost everything in the riot, including his hotel.

The white citizens used the riot to reaffirm their power over blacks through their hyperviolent destruction. The reason for this is the unique circumstance of Greenwood as an economic center for black businesses in the United States. Before the riot, the neighborhood was also known as Black Wall Street. Unlike so many black enclaves in the country, Greenwood had a thriving business district with a newspaper, movie theater, and a large hotel that served blacks from all over the country as they passed through Tulsa. The money of Tulsa's black population was a direct threat to the structures of meaning and values of white supremacist Christianity that thrived on affirming its superiority over all nonwhites, but particularly over African-Americans. The need to counterbalance the cosmoses of Tulsa was necessary for the maintenance of white power. This is why, even a week after the riot, the city required identification cards be carried by black people on the street (like the yellow stars worn by Jews, or even more aptly, the tags worn by slaves when they left the plantation) in order to regulate and reassert white dominance as a way of being in Tulsa.

The events of the riot lead to questions about the relationship between the black and white residents of Tulsa that cannot be unilaterally answered by the particular events of May 31 and June 1. The explosion of violence and the decimation of the black neighborhood in Tulsa were not solely due to the events surrounding the possible hanging of Dick Rowland. The Tulsa Race Riot was an act of religious expression necessitated by the white community not receiving the required retribution it sought for the societal taboo of a black man assaulting a white woman. Whether Dick Rowland legally committed a crime or not, he offended the laws of white supremacist Christianity. These unwritten rules established the decorum of life in Tulsa. The white community of Tulsa operated from a space where ultimacy was found in the whiteness of their skin. They might have professed to be Christian, secular, or some other form of believer on the religious spectrum, but the actions in Tulsa show a different divine expression that dominated the social structures within the city.

The events of Tulsa demonstrate the imperialism of the god of space by showing how the white citizens of the city revolted when their black neighbors took a stand to save the life of Rowland.[22] This act of defiance could not and would not be tolerated in a system of white consciousness where ultimacy was found within the ontology of white supremacy. In addition to this, white society was denied its performative ritual of lynching by the arrival of the blacks to stop the lynching. The denial of Rowland's blood for the tainting of Page's purity necessitated the riot due to the operations of white supremacist Christianity. To deny the believers their due justice for the assault on a white woman's purity was a direct insult to the god of white supremacy. The denial of the ritual of sacrifice as performed in the lynching of Rowland is what led to the ecstatic explosion of the religious in the form of rioting.[23] The violence was a transcendent moment in the life of the white community. The expressiveness of meaning found in the communal violence connected the people to the god of white supremacy by fulfilling its need for the destruction of other space.[24] Quite literally, the god of white supremacy desired the destruction of black bodies and black materiality in the form of houses, businesses, and any objects that could call into question the greatness of white supremacy's divine power.

The denial of Dick Rowland as a sacral offering through lynching caused a crisis moment in the collective psyche of white supremacy. Because the creative force of lynching was denied, the holy energy had to be redirected into the closest agent of regeneration. Without satisfaction, the ultimacy of the white God could not truly be ultimate. Another way to understand the events in Tulsa is in its relationship to *Kristallnacht*. In this situation, the people of Germany were denied the public justice deemed necessary by a Jew murdering a Nazi official. The people of Germany gained satisfaction by attacking the Jews in Germany, their businesses, and their synagogues on a mass scale to ensure that the order of things was not disrupted. White supremacist Christianity necessitates the continual reassertion of the divine order, and as a result, any event that questions these cosmic truths must be met with a counterforce that reasserts and further solidifies the place of the demonic divine.

The aftermath of the transcendental violence in Tulsa did not quell the need to honor the god of white supremacy. Two months after the riot, the citizens of Tulsa had a guest speaker in the convention center, which had until shortly before been used to detain blacks. The speaker was a minister from Georgia, who spoke on behalf of the Ku Klux Klan during the business week. In his speech, quoted in *The Chicago Defender*, the Klan minister said:

"A white man is a white man," thundered the speaker, "whether he lives in New Jersey, Indiana, Kansas, Illinois, Oklahoma, or Georgia. And a white man's job is see that civilization comes under the dominion of no inferior race so long as he lives."

IN *THE CHICAGO DEFENDER*'S DESCRIPTION OF THE SCENE,

No interruptions marred the address, the large audiences remaining quiet and attentive during the speech. Several city officials gave their approval of the meeting by stopping other duties to attend to. Dr. Ridley, who declared he was an "imperial elder" in the Klan, insisted that he was not a paid lecturer of that organization, but was spending his vacation "between Sundays" speaking for it.[25]

Almost three months after the horrors of what could only be described as a white riot, the people of Tulsa were still living into the destructive religiosity that perpetuated white power. The belief of white dominance over all races was consistent throughout white society, at the time of this speech, and was evidenced through the Western world's subjugation of the vast majority of the planet through colonizing governments. As the minister stated in his address, it was held to be the job of the white race to subdue all other races in order to assure the preservation of civilization. This line of thinking directly connects to the imperialism of the god of space. The divine power of the god of white supremacy operates through the need to prove white supremacist Christianity's ultimacy over all other space.

In arguing for the preservation of civilization, the minister is connecting the idea of god's creation to the appointment of white people as civilization's purveyors. In this way, the Tulsa riot can also be seen as the white people of Tulsa cutting the weeds that overtook creation and threatened the natural, god-ordained balance of creation. The destruction of Black Wall Street was not only the result of unfortunate events, but can be seen as a sacrifice of expiation to the white God in order to atone for allowing black people to attain a degree of power in the city that was seemingly choking out the god-ordained power of whites. In this way, the white riot that destroyed Black Wall Street was a reassertion of god's will.

WORSHIP AT THE TREE

In the second piece of this chapter, I turn to how the demonic operated through the mutilation of black bodies during the era of lynching. The practice of lynching started during the Reconstruction era. This is not to say that other forms of mob justice were not practiced before the Civil War; however, what is envisioned as lynching in the form of hanging took shape after the war. In the years of Reconstruction, the act of lynching did not necessarily mean attacks on nonwhites, but as whites resolidified control of the former Confederate states after Reconstruction, lynching became associated more and more with vigilante justice against blacks.[26] In fact, in the decades following the era of Reconstruction, an estimated 4,697 people were lynched in the United States. At least 3,344 victims were Americans of African descent, which means at least 71% of the victims were considered black.[27] To compound this problem, as the country moved farther away from the years of the Civil War, lynching became a form of punishment predominantly used against blacks. This does not mean that lynching was not used against others, as the lynching of Leo Frank in 1915 attests[28]—and yet, by the 1930s, the term "lynching" implied black victims.[29] What becomes clear in the solidification of lynching in the form of white mob violence against blacks is the transition of lynching to an expression of white power using violence to maintain a societal order of whites against and over nonwhites, particularly in this instance focused on black Americans. The goal of lynching, as read through a religious lens, is the sacrificial maintenance of power, much in the same way the Romans used crucifixion to maintain order at the periphery of the empire in the time of Jesus of Nazareth. To break down lynching to its symbolic core, that is, beyond the historical and statistical jargon, unveils its aesthetic quality as essential to the white supremacist faith.

The symbolic nature of lynching, as with each of the historical events discussed within this text, is important precisely because of its mythological substance. In her article "Nooses in Public Spaces: A Womanist Critique of Lynching—A 21st Century Ethical Dilemma," Angela D. Sims states, "To examine the causes of lynching from both historical and contemporary perspectives is one way to articulate the theological-ethical implications associated with Southern horrors as well as to assess its devastating effects."[30] Lynching is not simply an event or series of events that took place long ago in a time when the United States was a racist nation; instead, it is necessary to view the symbolic history of lynching as more of a theo-historical moment in the creation of white supremacist Christianity, wherein black bodies are sacrificed for the sanctification of white flesh in order to instill the cultural and structural beliefs that equate whiteness with godliness. To view lynching in this sort of way also means to question the way in which Christian theology is perceived and operates in the context of white supremacy throughout the Western-controlled world, and particularly the United States. Lynching—like the race-based legacies of Indian removal, chattel slavery, and the persecution of Catholics, Jews, and persons from Asia and the Middle East—reveals an aspect of the soul of the United States and should be viewed in relation to its ritualistic meanings.[31] Deciphering the symbolic messages of white supremacy and its functions in the moral/social structure of white society is key to understanding the particular shape that Christianity has taken in the United States, and without an analysis that takes seriously this theo-historical narrative, there will not be opportunities of engaging the demonic nature of the religiosity exposed in lynching.

Admittedly, most people envision lynching as being an act of white-robed men in the cover of darkness, but this was rarely the case and was not the reality with the lynch mob in Marion, Indiana. On August 7, 1930, two black men named Thomas Schipp and Abe Smith were lynched in front of the Marion County courthouse for the alleged murder of Claude Deeter (a white man) and the alleged assault of a white woman named Mary Ball.[32] Newspapers in Chicago reported as many as 5,000 spectators gathered around the courthouse to witness the beating, mutilation, and hanging of both Schipp and Smith.[33]

While this event might not be particularly surprising to a student of U.S. history, the symbolic and sacral meanings of lynching in America are often ignored or misperceived by the observing eye of whites and left to the devices of black scholars to investigate. The case of the lynching of Schipp and Smith is forever imprinted in U.S. history through a widely distributed picture of the lynching scene that shows their battered and bruised bodies hanging from the courthouse tree, surrounded by white sightseers and revelers. As one gazes at the horrifying scene, the reality of two Americas takes shape. The first is of a black America where the accused can be humiliated and murdered simply for being black in America. As the *New York Amsterdam News* said on August 27, 1930, "every fair-minded person will admit that in the United States a colored man is lynched for the crime of being a Negro."[34] A reality whites (including myself) cannot fully understand is the legacy of the continual existential assault against blacks, as well as other nonwhites, through the disposable nature of their being in the United States. Blacks are used, abused,

Figure 4.1 Marion Lynching. August 7, 1930. Used by the permission of the Indiana Historical Society. *Source*: Lawrence H. Beitler, *Marion Lynching*, 1930, Indiana Historical Society.

and killed for the explicit benefits of whites, and there is no further proof needed than the picture of the Marion lynching which was sold to whites as a souvenir of the momentous occasion in a town that had never had the honor of lynching a Negro.[35] As Harvey Young, in his article "The Black Body as Souvenir in American Lynching," states:

> On the scheduled day and at the appointed hour, scores of spectators would assemble to witness the public staging of vengeance acted upon the accused by the victim or the victim's family, the prolonged torture of the accused by the lynching organizers, the lynching (by burning, hanging, or shooting) of the accused, and the dismemberment of the accused's body into souvenirs. As public performances, lynchings far surpassed all other forms of entertainment in terms of their ability to attract an audience and the complexity of their narratives. A lynching was an event—something not to be missed.[36]

The bodies of Schipp and Smith acted as sacred symbols of the mundane character of white supremacist Christianity. To put this another way, James H. Madison states "From the moment the mob broke through the jail doors Smith and Schipp became symbols of an evil that had to be destroyed, wiped away, purified by the ritual of lynching."[37] To understand lynching in a symbolic manner is to understand it as a sacrifice to the god of whiteness who gives whites dominion over all creation for the betterment of white race; therefore, the physical act of lynching is by no means mundane in any sense. One needs take a wide view of the lynching scene that does not focus on Schipp and Smith, but rather on the white crowd. This refocusing starts to reveal the real character of whiteness in America. In this picture are the freely exposed and joyous faces of white men and women who do not fear legal recourse because vigilante justice by whites against nonwhites does not warrant legal action. The demonic can be found by not looking at the picture for what it presents at the surface level, but rather digging deeper into the symbolic level of white power for the sake and propagation of white power.

By the nature of U.S. demographics, all the people in this picture—including a couple on the left who are expecting a child, the older woman looking over her shoulder, or the man with the tattooed arm pointing at Schipp and Smith—are probably educated in the Christian tradition. This does not mean that everyone who witnessed the lynching in Marion, Indiana, on August 7, 1930 was a religiously devout Christian, but they were raised and lived in a society permeated by the symbolism and doctrine of Christianity.[38] What I argue can be seen in this picture is the destructive creativity of a demonic Christianity that is shaped and maintained through the elevation of whiteness to a divine status and a religious fervor that prioritizes white over nonwhite by providing ultimate meaning to the fortunate few who embody the proper class, faith, gender, and pigment of the demonic divine. This is the second

America, where white life is valued and superimposed over and against all others.

The dichotomy of two Americas is found in the drive toward ultimacy found in the god of white supremacy. In attending the lynching of Schipp and Smith, the spectators participated in a religious spectacle that provided meaning to everyone who witnessed the ghastly event. The power of white supremacist Christianity revealed itself to the members of the crowd by demonstrating the power of their god as evidenced in the dangling black bodies. Indeed, the strange fruit of lynching cast into nonbeing blacks and others during the era of lynching, but it also revealed the daily workings of the god of white supremacy among its followers. The power of lynching reminded the community of whites of the power of their divine connection to the god of white supremacy.

The indelible image of the lynching of Schipp and Smith shows the gathering of a white mob in order to perform a ritual of white faith. The execution of this common cause for the betterment of the white race enabled whites of all classes to come together. "Lynching served to intimidate blacks who might have challenged the white power structure; by demonstrating their capacity for deadly violence, as well as the ineffectiveness of federal measures to stop them, whites warned blacks not to seek changes in the established social."[39] This common goal of proving the power of whiteness necessitated the sacrifice of black bodies for the continuation of a white society. This societal power demanded maintenance higher than the legal powers of the federal government that formally outlaws the extralegal activities of white mobs; the lawmakers of U.S. government at all levels answered to the higher power of white supremacist Christianity before the laws of the land that supposedly dictated their actions time and again. Even law enforcement, who are commissioned to protect all persons, including those who are imprisoned, often were not willing to carry out their duties in order to protect black suspects in the face of a white mob, particularly in cases when the mob desired to lynch a black man for an alleged assault against a white women.[40] In fact, in times when a black man was accused of raping a white women and the white community felt the act of lynching was necessary, officers of the law have been rumored to incite the crowd, as was the case in the events that led to the lynching of Schipp and Smith.[41] In this respect, the act of social violence in the form of lynching does not need the black body that is to be hung to actually be the perpetrator of any kind of crime because lynching is a performance of the act of social control.[42]

The creation of a religious society based on the beliefs of white supremacy and the control of nonwhites is shown in the lynching of over 3,000 black persons, including Schipp and Smith, but what is the theological message transmitted by the belief of white structures that necessitates the destruction of nonwhite bodies? The communities of lynching were steeped in the Christian tradition that explicitly claims the principle that all human bodies are made in *imago dei*, but local white churches generally did not protest the demonic warping of this doctrine to apply only to whites. It was commonplace in the aftermath of a lynching for the local religious authorities to remain silent, and through their silence, aid in the perpetuation of white supremacy. An example of enabling lynching is the statistics that show some southern counties, like Sumter County, Alabama, had an exceptionally high participation in white churches at the time a lynching occurred in the community.[43] This community of churchgoing folk found it necessary to lynch a black man, and the churches in the community remained silent. Oftentimes, clergy justified their silence in the aftermath of lynchings by saying that even though the participants were members of their congregations, they disavowed any responsibility for community issues outside the church.[44] These men of God viewed their calling as only to the daily functions of the church and not to the care of all men's souls.

The response of the local church is not the whole story surrounding ecclesial reaction to lynching. Like many other social issues, the national offices of many denominations repeatedly condemned the act of lynching and called on their members to protest the murder of black men by white mobs. What is the difference between the local and national churches? What the national churches (as well as government officials) failed to recognize, in trying to curb lynching violence, is that there is a significant difference between formal church theology—based on dogma and doctrine—and cultural theology, which oftentimes is a better measure of the theological underpinnings of members of the local church.[45] The creation of dogma and doctrine, in instances like the four ecumenical councils or church conferences, has little bearing on the functionality of the popular religious beliefs of the masses who oftentimes use religion to justify their actions and beliefs or who demand the separation of faith matters from everyday affairs in order to bifurcate their discordant social anchors from the religious tenets of their denominations. In actuality, popular theology works to maintain social power through the guise of religious meaning.

Through the work of cultural theology, white persons created a system of meaning; in order to give clarity to the world, white supremacist Christianity used faith systems to deny the humanness of black people.[46] This is precisely how lynching came to operate as a religious spectacle. In the act of destroying black bodies, whites found social and individual meaning in the common beliefs of the superiority of whites through the popularly constructed mores of Christianity over and against all other forms of –ness.

In finding meaning through the spectacle of lynching, it is appropriate to return to its ritualized nature through the way mob violence changed the destiny of the lynching community. Children were removed from school for the higher learning of white supremacy,[47] much as *The Education for Death* described the higher learning of Nazism.[48] Through the practice of white fulfillment in black destruction, the importance of lynching to the community was not lost on the adults, who used lynching as a catechetical moment for future generations. Angela D. Sims describes it this way:

> White males gathered to participate in a sacrificial ritual condoned by members of their respective communities. Lynching spectators gathered to perpetuate a practice whose existence depended on the passing down of hatred from one generation to the next. They lynched because they could, without fear of retaliation, kill at will.[49]

This quote reveals a significant reality of lynching culture that not only demonstrates the freedom of whites to move and act freely within society, but also the necessity of passing down "traditions," in the same way Christian churches require congregations to commit to teaching those who are baptized the dogmas and doctrines of their faith system. Lynching required the indoctrination of hatred in successive generations to ensure the continuation of white supremacy.

Lynching became a sacralized way of maintaining the community dynamics to protect the system of white supremacist Christianity against any form of social assault. In this way, lynching can be read through a Girardian lens to comprehend how the lynching of a black body could be a sacred ritual within the body of whiteness. René Girard in *Violence and the Sacred* sets up an understanding of sacrifice not based on the structure of a priest offering a gift to a deity.[50] Girard's idea of sacrifice is based on the way in which societies use the sacrifice of an outsider to solve the collective unrest.[51] This framing of sacrifice turns the ritual of lynching from envisioning it as a sort of burnt offering to a deity into the way white supremacist Christianity maintains social control and order. The lynching of Schipp and Smith represented Girard's notion of sacrifice in which "the function of sacrifice is to quell violence within the community and to prevent conflicts from erupting."[52] Their deaths at the hands of the white people of Marion symbolized the acting out of the will of god as a just act to provide satisfaction for what was considered to be more than just the individual crimes of murder and rape. The ultimacy of whiteness made Schipp and Smith's accused actions a crime against the community of the god of white supremacy. For this reason, the collective act of violence as performed in the lynching of two black men acted as the transference of a collective sin in order to prevent further violence.[53]

In comparing the lynching of Schipp and Smith to the events in Tulsa, one can better understand the two different paths through Girard's idea of sacrifice. In Marion, Indiana, the "outsiders" were sacrificed to maintain social order and avoid the eruption of further violence. The events in Tulsa were different because they lacked a centralized release of sacred violence. The white community of Tulsa perceived the actions of Rowland through collective victimization. In this framework, the Girardian understanding of sacrifice would require the sacrifice of an object that would take on the collective sin of the black community against the whites of Tulsa. Girard frames it this way: "A single victim can be substituted for all the potential victims, for all the enemy brothers that each member is striving to banish from the community; he can be substituted, in fact, for each and every member of the community."[54] The focusing of communal attention onto one victim would have enabled the community to exert their violent rage as a communal act, but with the denial of this ritual, the white community turned to the whole of the black community of Tulsa. While the denial of sacrifice in Tulsa led to the explosion of violence against the whole black community, in Marion, the ritual act of lynching enabled the community to restore the natural order by the sacrifice of Schipp and Smith. The community's ability to transfer all its angst on two individuals provided the white spectators a connection to the power of meaning found in the ultimacy of whiteness.

Tillich's concept of the demonic pinpoints here the discordant nature of being that is found in the despairing reality of estrangement. As people seek meaning in their lives, the goal is strictly to find said meaning, but at what cost? As Tillich argues, finding meaning in finite objects can, and often does, lead to destructive patterns of existence. This is exactly what we find in the events leading to the lynching in Marion. Returning to the image of the white lynch mob and the mangled bodies of Schipp and Smith, one can see the demonic nature of white supremacy in action. The indelible image depicts the ritualized nature of lynching that Harvey Young describes, but unlike his work, this image is a clear religious expression. The act of lynching is an ecstatic act of violence perpetuated by a group or mob that seeks extralegal justice against a small number of persons who are rendered defenseless by the sheer ratio of mob to victims. As was earlier explained, lynching is not solely the act of hanging a person by the use of rope from an elevation where they would suffocate or break their neck; rather, lynching is an explosion of violence that takes the shape of a mob-based revenge that can manifest in many different forms, the most common of which is burning or hanging.

To continue the theme of spectacle, Charles Mills argues that lynching often turned into community gatherings in which families gathered together in a celebratory mood to witness the events of the day and would ensure that they stayed to the end of the festivities to obtain a keepsake or token of the momentous occasion, like a piece of clothing from the victim or a part of the tree or rope, and the most prized possessions were dismembered remains of the black victim.[55] As with other aspects of the religiosity of lynching, again, there is a religious motif to the collection of these relics that clearly holds the same sort of religious meaning to be desired by so many members of a lynch mob which makes a clear correlation between the collection of lynching mementos and the desire of devout Christians in previous centuries to collect clothing or body parts of the saints or even fragments of the true cross.

This particular point is too important to be missed if one is to understand the operative and mythical nature of white supremacy in the United States. The lynching relics are tangible pieces of the faith system and symbolically connect the white actors through a communal act, in much the same way the use of bread and wine brings together believers on Sunday morning. The events that took place in Marion exemplify lynchings that took place across the Midwestern and southern states. The people of Marion and the surrounding countryside gathered at the center of town to witness the lynching of Schipp and Smith through the performative motif of extralegal murder, and when the sacrifice for the sake of white power and order was complete, the supposed crowd of 5,000 clamored for relics of the lynching or mementos, like photos, to remind them of the day. In fact, accounts have been given that the people of Marion made sure to take strips of clothing from Schipp and Smith and to cut off pieces of the bark from the lynching tree.[56] Madison assessed the drive for relics in this way:

> Why people would want to spend 50 cents to purchase one of Beitler's souvenirs is uncertain. But they did, in Marion, and across America, where lynchings often resulted in photographs and even postcards of the gruesome event. Like others, the Marion photograph was a keepsake, of course, a marker of a spectacular occurrence. Perhaps some also wanted to own the photograph as a reassurance of white supremacy and of race solidarity in the face of any perceived black threat, a talisman against murder or rape or inappropriate crossing of the color line. One copy of Beitler's photograph ended up under glass, double matted and framed. Someone inscribed on the inner mat in pencil 'Bo pointin to his niga.' And between the mat and the glass were placed locks of hair thought to be either Shipp's or Smith's.[57]

While this whole quote by Madison is terrifying and disturbing, there is the collection of all themes in one piece right at the end. The affirmation of one's whiteness was so essential to their ontological meaning that the mob found it necessary to take a copy of Beitler's picture and frame it with a lock of hair from either Schipp or Smith imbedded in the frame, as a family would take a picture and memento from a vacation and put them together. Beitler's picture helped artificially enforce the ecstatic power of white faith by providing a historical recourse for blacks of what would happen if they became a perceived threat to whites, but also, Beitler's picture reinscribed for the white faithful their dominion over the beasts of the land. This mentality of taming the Negro

beast is clearly witnessed in the inscription attributed to the man in the middle
of the picture "pointin to his niga."[58]

James Cone also recognizes the importance of lynching acting as a spectacle of white space to ensure the consolidation white supremacy within the
community. By attending a lynching event, the whole white community would
be reaffirmed in the power of the white God through the sacrifice of black
bodies. This made the participation of all in attendance a necessity because of
lynching's ability not only to demonstrate power, but also to provide a direct
connection to the white God through the participation of all in attendance. "It
was a family affair, a ritual celebration of white supremacy, where women
and children were burning black flesh and cutting off genitals, fingers, toes,
and ears as souvenirs. Postcards were made from the photographs taken of
black victims with white lynchers and onlookers smiling as they struck a pose
for the camera."[59] While Cone does not explicitly reference the lynching in
Marion, this quote clearly connects to the photograph discussed previously.
The people of Marion were active participants in the regeneration of white
power through the lynching of two black men. Lynching was never just a
simple act of corporal punishment carried out through extralegal means; it
was the white community's way of connecting with their white God.

THE PRESERVATION OF WHITE SPACE

In the final piece of this chapter, I focus on an aspect of segregative housing policy in the city of Detroit during the New Deal era. Like the previous
two pieces of this chapter, the history of federally funded segregative housing practice is relatively unknown within the mythos of the United States.
Detroit, in particular, has a long history of designing neighborhoods based
on the drive for racial homogeneity, which even today follows the legally
defunct practice of separate-but-equal as established by *Plessy v. Ferguson*.
But what drove the city to use the racially based housing practices that continue to plague the city today and are a root problem impacting the economy,
deteriorating school system, and concentration of violent crime within the
city limits of modern Detroit?

The years surrounding World War II were an economic boom for the
city of Detroit. The city grew exponentially due to the prosperity from the
concentration of heavy industry in metropolitan Detroit.[60] As a result of the
expansion of economic freedom, particularly in the white ethnic sections of
the city, a shift began to occur among the white population. The accumulation
of wealth instituted a shift in community alignments among the ethnic whites
that during this time changed the way they identified themselves based on
class and their whiteness and less on their ethnic and immigrant status.[61] This

change in self-identity reshaped the Detroit housing market as former ethnic communities, which had oftentimes shared space with blacks, abandoned these dwellings to move to areas of the city with perceived higher social status. The result of this shift to racially identified housing made it difficult for blacks to find housing when they moved to the city for blue-collar jobs in the automotive and, later, the war industry. The only housing options available were dangerously overpopulated neighborhoods, like Paradise Valley near downtown Detroit.

The industrial shift to the construction of war goods brought substantial military contracts to the city and resulted in rapid economic expansion and the need for single-family homes. The creation of the Federal Housing Authority (FHA) in 1934 enabled the push for single-family homes throughout the city of Detroit, particularly as more blue-collar families sought jobs at city factories, through federally backed mortgages.[62] As white families used these federal funds to move out of the overpopulated neighborhoods downtown, the federal government systematically created policies to deny these rights to black workers by requiring racial homogeneity in FHA—backed housing developments and simultaneously considering black neighborhoods unsuitable for housing loans. In his article for *The Atlantic* entitled "The Case for Reparations," Ta-Nehisi Coates says:

> The FHA insured private mortgages causing a drop in interest rates and a decline in the size of the down payment required to buy a house. But an insured was not possible for Clyde Ross [an African-American male]. The FHA had adopted a system of maps that rated neighborhoods according to their perceived stability. On the maps, green areas, rated 'A,' indicated 'in demand' neighborhoods that as on appraiser put it, lacked 'a single foreigner or Negro.' These neighborhoods were considered excellent prospects for insurance. Neighborhoods where black people live were rated 'D' and were usually considered ineligible for FHA backing. They were colored in red. Neither the percentage of black people living there nor their social class mattered. Black people were viewed as a contagion. Redlining went beyond FHA-backed loans and spread to the entire mortgage industry, which was already rife with racism, excluding black people from most legitimate means of obtaining a mortgage.[63]

In essence, the FHA policy toward housing loans inherently carried a racist structure. This sort of institutional racism puts the lie to the argument that proclaims racism is solely individual. On the level of housing policies based on racial makeup of the neighborhoods, the federal government established its funding practices to systematically carry out an apartheid-like treatment of citizens that the U.S. government had declared equal by the Fourteenth Amendment to the U.S. Constitution almost eighty years earlier.

The FHA policy of not lending to African-Americans was staunchly fought in Detroit by the inhabitants of the E-W area on the far north side of the city. This enclave on the outskirts of the city became a bastion for poor blacks that desired to leave the slums of the areas like Paradise Valley near downtown Detroit, since it was close enough to work in the industrial centers.[64] This neighborhood acted as an anomaly in the city in the decades prior to World War II because of its black and white tenants. Both racial groups came together here from the same poor economic standing to acquire a piece of land where they could build their own home. The poor families would purchase the land and build their homes with whatever materials they could afford from their disposable income, and oftentimes this meant a continual cycle of substandard housing. At the time the original residents moved to the E-W area, the land was predominantly uninhabited, and the city did not concern itself with the lack of adequate housing. This policy changed as the need for housing increased during the war, and developers sought to build on the land surrounding the neighborhood. By the 1940s, the Federal Housing Administration and the city of Detroit viewed E-W as a blight on the economic prospects of the city.[65] By this time, the FHA-lending maps considered the E-W area to be unsuitable for federal support and deemed any lands directly surrounding E-W to also be unsuitable for development. This classification as a redlined area by the FHA was an impediment to white business developers who considered the northern border of the city an opportune pace to build middle-class housing because of its accessibility to downtown.[66] In 1940, a white developer sought permission to build FHA homes bordering E-W and was denied access to federal funds due to the proximity of black neighborhoods; in order to appease the federal lenders, the developer constructed a wall to formally and physically segregate the black dwellings from the new white housing. The wall stood at a foot thick and six-feet high and spanned a mile to delineate the racialized neighborhoods.

This wall signified to the black residents of Detroit, and in particular of E-W, how the city and the federal government viewed them.

The government would guarantee repayment to any bank who loaned money for homebuilding. It was an over-simplified statement, but that's how the home-seekers in the Eight Mile area explained the Federal Housing Administration Act, and they were jubilant.

As industry absorbed the unemployed, applications were resubmitted to banks for loans. White neighborhoods now occupied areas from Greenlawn to Livernois, north and south of Pembroke. The latest development for whites began at Mendota and had progressed as far as Meyers Road.

'Homes to the east of us, homes to the south of us, homes to the west of us, but nothing for us,' was the way the home-seekers summed it up.

. . .

'We talked with the man who is head of the developing company. He said the wall is on HIS [*sic*] property and there wasn't anything we could do about it. He further said that he was forced to shut off the view of our dilapidated houses to increase his chances of selling those homes on Mendota. Those homes are F.H.A. approved too.'

So the six-foot concrete wall remained on the line of the alley at the rear of Birwood. But the Carver Progressive Club members had been slapped in the face before, and this, though humiliating, did not faze them.[67]

The community of E-W recognized the disparities of the housing policies affecting the area around them, and as black residents, they did not have access to these opportunities because the color of their skin meant they were not suitable candidates. In addition, when the community organization inquired about the construction of the wall bordering Mendota and Birwood, they were tersely told by the white developer that their mere presence in the area made it impossible to sell homes without the construction of the wall to block the sight of blacks, as well as the accessibility to blacks of the new white houses that would follow the approval of the FHA loans for new construction. The man made it clear through his views of the black neighborhood that the problem was the black people, and this reality was compounded by the government's refusal to accept E-W as an acceptable community for housing loans, while at the same time enabling white communities to blossom and to eventually surround the E-W neighborhood on the east, south, and west when the blacks of E-W already had to contend with segregationist housing practices on the north side of Eight Mile in the suburban cities bordering Detroit. The unsatisfactory conditions of housing in E-W were indeed problematic to the well-being of its inhabitants, and the government could have alleviated this issue through admission of the neighborhood into the FHA loan program, but the condition of the houses was not the ultimate concern for their white neighbors. The true concern was the presence of black bodies and the perception of blackness as something unclean and inherently unworthy to reside in proximity to white bodies.

The residents of E-W were deemed as not worthy of federal backing not because of their merits, like employability or credit worthiness, but rather because of the pigmentation of their skin. This realization led the residents of E-W to protest the construction of the wall and to lobby the Franklin Delano Roosevelt administration to overturn the FHA decision to deny federal funds to loan applicants in black neighborhoods. The lobbying for the expansion of FHA loans was rebuffed by the government and justified by the perceived unsuitability of building in a black neighborhood.[68]

In response to the FHA decision to not grant E-W acceptable lending status, residents of the neighborhood organized a civic organization to continue to put pressure on New Deal liberals in Washington, D.C. to expand social programs, like housing loans, to the E-W area.[69] During their fight with FHA to gain access to loans, developers argued that the land in E-W should be repurposed in order to remove the slum housing projects encircled by white neighbors.[70] Federal segregationist housing policies aided attempts to remove blacks for the betterment of the city, that is, the white sections of the city.

For three years, the civic organizations representing E-W continued to lobby the FHA for the reclassification of the neighborhood, and even though the director of the FHA was sympathetic to their cause, he committed the FHA to a policy of separate-but-equal that never in actuality led to equal treatment under the law.[71] Finally, in 1943, the FHA director agreed to visit the neighborhood to determine if the area was suitable for housing loans, but white developers and white civic organizations strongly lobbied against the lifting of the lending ban because of their fears that black neighbors would decrease the value of the surrounding housing projects.[72] In addition, the white housing developers believed that to expand housing rights to blacks would limit their ability to eventually acquire the land for more white middle-class projects.[73] To prove their argument, the white civic organizations cited a study of the E-W area by Marvel Daines in *Be It Ever So Tumbled* that described E-W.

> We ask, what if none of these plans ever comes to fruition? Are we to endure the unhealthful, unsightly, and uneconomic menace of this neighborhood until the shacks fall into ruins because of their own instability?
>
> We leave the solving of this problem up to the reader. But try to see through the eyes of the colored man. He wants a decent place to live—just as you and I. He wants a decent job, and an opportunity to make something of himself. Yet the prayer of the Dark Brother is a humble one . . . [74]

While this quote by Daines shows what could be a genuine concern for the black residents of E-W, the phrasing shows a theological worldview that undermines the good-natured concern espoused. To look beyond the surface meaning of trying to find adequate housing and jobs for the black residents reveals the belief of E-W's white neighbors that the best possibility would be for them to remove the blackness from among their midst. The true issue is not the condition of housing or unemployment; rather, the black body seemingly operates as a menace to white prosperity. None of the proposals submitted in *Be It Ever So Tumbled* seriously considered the redevelopment of the area for its black residents, which would seem to be the most logical option. An obvious reason for not considering rehabilitation was the white desire for the destruction of black space among them.

The white civic groups that included white developers argued for the removal of the black residents of E-W, and as an attempt at a compromise, they agreed that housing should be constructed for the displaced black families near the industrial complexes.[75] The reality is that while the white organizers feigned concern for the black residents of E-W, their primary motive was the removal of a contagion that could only be viewed as harmful to their prospects. By removing the black virus, the white residents and developers could stop worrying about the destruction of housing values and physical property.

Along with the white developers, the city desired the removal of the black families in order to construct an airport that was close to downtown.[76] The E-W area was one of many areas considered by the city for the construction of the airport, including uninhabited lots on the west side of the town, but the city viewed the E-W area as preferable due to what they presumed would be little political resistance. The reason for this belief was that the city believed investors would accept the plan in order to remove the black housing options near the new white neighborhoods. Another positive to choosing this site was the lack of political capital held by poor blacks in the city. The city made a calculated decision to rely on white developers who had the money and influence in the city to get the airport built at E-W, even against significant opposition of the black community. The city's political calculation failed to garner the requisite support of white residents and builders who viewed the construction of the airport as a threat to further middle-class neighborhoods.[77] As a way to appease the white residents near E-W, the city abandoned its plan for an airport and focused on removing the black residents to repurpose the land for white construction. At any other time in the history of Detroit, the removal of black families from E-W might have been possible, but this was during World War II, when the military-industrial complex required the vast majority of resources to be committed to the war effort.[78] As result of the war, the city and the Federal Housing Administration proposed building temporary war industry homes in the E-W area. As a compromise with the residents of E-W, the FHA agreed to grant loan status to E-W as long as war housing could be built on vacant or repossessed lots. With this agreement, the city built 600 temporary homes in E-W, and the black residents received federal backing for housing loans.

In the decade after the wall was created to satisfy the housing regulators' segregationist housing policies, the E-W area saw the construction of 1,500 new single-family homes for black residents. Soon after, black residents integrated the white housing complexes, as well.[79] In fact, twenty years after the construction of the wall, at least 88% of the homes in E-W were owner occupied. And yet, the racially exclusive policies of the Federal Housing Administration did not significantly change in other parts of the country.[80] These refusals to alter housing policies meant other black neighborhoods, in Detroit and across the country, were incapable of receiving the capital to redevelop badly overpopulated and dilapidated housing.[81] Ultimately, the

FHA-lending practices benefited the white lower class in its efforts to become middle class, while leaving blacks to create an existence without equal protection and rights.

The creation of the E-W wall in 1940 signified the formalization of federal separate-but-equal policies in Detroit that had also governed the rest of the country ever since *Plessy v. Ferguson*, but this wall meant so much more than the creation of two distinct neighborhoods. The wall codified the belief in the inferiority of blacks to the point that it felt necessary to whites to create a physical barrier between the perceived contagion of black bodies and the natural sanctity of the white form. This wall, like all walls, was designed to keep out something, like the walls of a home are constructed to create a refuge from the outside world; the E-W wall was built to protect the white communities from the danger of blackness.

While the wall only served a tangible purpose for a few years, its symbolic reality lives on as the wall still stands as a reminder of local and federal support of racial policies that popular U.S. history only admits took place in the Jim/Jane Crow south. White supremacist Christianity needs the backing of structural systems, like housing policies, to consolidate the rewards of whites and to make sure that no nonwhites partake in the riches of the white God. In this way, whiteness operates as the antithesis of empathy by creating conditions where whites can determine the trajectory of life based on the pigmentation of one's skin. Yes, some nonwhites can break the chains of race-based economic oppression, but even then a glass ceiling is placed on their achievements in order to make sure that blacks never can attain the equality that even Jim/Jane Crow officially proclaimed, let alone the full equality the United States. Constitution gives through the Fourteenth Amendment. Again, the creation of the E-W wall illustrated the limits of the legal system in the face of a popular theology, inscribed through the traditions of Christianity, that placed the value of white civilization and power as the ultimate concern of American society. The power of white supremacist faith is that it brings together all those who benefit from its majesty into a common destiny that defines freedom through the propagation of the white race and the cosmic battle against the impurities of blackness.

The construction of the wall ensured the protection of whites within Detroit by guaranteeing the separation of the races through the federal housing code. As with the use of walls to separate Jews from Christians in medieval Europe and Nazi Germany, the federal government realized the importance of safeguarding whites from blacks. In this way, the government backed the theology of white supremacist Christianity by recognizing the importance of white purity and the need to eliminate the black threat from within its midst while white women and children slept in their beds. Unlike the citizens of Tulsa, the citizens of Detroit used the federal government to protect them from the black menace. This would not be necessary unless the whites of Detroit feared the tainting effects of blackness. Whites in Detroit understood themselves as connected to something beyond them: the power of whiteness.

To describe this situation another way, the E-W wall, as it stands today, goes by another name. In the city of Detroit, the wall is now known as the Wailing Wall. The wall signifies to the black community, which is now the vast majority of the whole city, a time when the city said they were not worthy opportunity on an equal basis with their white counterparts. As with the destruction of Black Wall Street in Tulsa and the lynch murder of Schipp and Smith in Marion, Indiana, the residents of E-W were sacrificed to and for the white God. Unlike the Tulsa riot and the Marion lynching, the victims did not experience physical death, but that does not mean there was not a social death as they were deemed unworthy of basic human rights or even the equal and adequate protection of self as their counterparts of the white race.[82] The wall is associated with wailing as a cry to God as the black people of this country have done since 1619 in the face of the white supremacist god and its community of believers. The Christian God whites used to propagate their white institutionalized faith through scripture and Christian tradition is the same God African-Americans have cried out to in order to save them from the demonry of whiteness.

CONCLUSION

The ontological power of white supremacy operates on a daily basis to protect white space and, through this, the white God. At the beginning of this chapter, I started by stating that the epistemology of whiteness had solidified white supremacy within the American psyche. The next step in developing the religion of white supremacy was to show how the preservation of white space developed the ontological nature of white supremacy. The historical investigation of the Tulsa Race Riot, the lynching of Abe Smith and Thomas Schipp in Marion, and the construction of the E-W wall in Detroit each prove the power of white space within their own historical context. These are certainly not the only examples of whites protecting the ultimacy of white supremacy in the United States, but they do show three different approaches to maintaining the power of the white God.

The riot in Tulsa proves within its historical place and time the insult given to the white God by the refusal of handing over Dick Rowland for lynching. The white people of Tulsa treated the denial of Rowland as a sacrifice to mean much more than the city's attempt at maintaining order. It was a direct insult to the white God that had to be rectified by even greater means. The presence of Black Wall Street became a symbol of black space as a direct threat to white space. Without the opportunity to lynch Rowland, Black Wall Street had to be eliminated to ensure the preservation of white space as the supreme power within the community. The violence that led to the destruction of the black neighborhood and the removal of the black people was a cosmic battle for the preservation of the white God.

Unlike Tulsa, the lynching in Marion performed as a coordinated ritual of sacrifice for the protection of white space, but also to honor the white God. Lynching events proved to be more than just the execution of predominantly black persons. As both Cone and Madison attest, there was a religious component to the participation of the whole white community. By participating in and collecting relics of the lynching event, the white people not only reasserted their power within the temporal realm, but also made themselves more pleasing to the white God. The relics held the power of memory and meaning for those who were lucky enough to attain such an artifact. In participating in the Marion lynching, the people of the surrounding area were able to reaffirm the power of white space not just in the present moment but also to future generations who lived in the shadow of the memorialized lynching event.

While both Tulsa and Marion used physical violence to preserve white space, Detroit used a very different and arguably more insidious approach to protect white space. The construction of the E-W wall by a real estate developer to ensure Federal Housing Authority support demonstrated the lengths the federal government was willing to go to preserve the power of whiteness. As will be seen in the next chapter, the government's commitment to the preservation of the white God makes sensible the creation of the wall to keep blacks away from good white folk. The wall also showed how the power of the white God reasserts itself in ways that are less direct than the use of physical violence. The preservation and protection of white space was the primary goal in the segregation of Detroit, but its effects can be seen in many northern cities, like Chicago, Milwaukee, and Philadelphia.

The Tulsa Race Riot of 1921 showed how the white community acts when its place in God's world is threatened. The power of denied sacrifice is plainly evident in the holy wrath of white supremacy wrought out on Black Wall Street. The dominant power of white being atoned for the insult against white honor by the denial of Dick Rowland's body by reinforcing the place of blackness in a white world through divine destruction. In Tulsa, the necessity to prove white space was not achieved by the desire to lynch Rowland. White space (as represented by the mythical purity of white women) did not receive satisfaction for the transgression of blackness into sacred space. What happened in Tulsa is religious violence to atone for the denial of a righteous sacrifice to reaffirm the holiness of the white God. The unleashing of widespread violence throughout the black neighborhood of Tulsa was an act of sacred violence to ensure the power of white supremacy. The invasion of Black Wall Street was a pogrom very much in line with the countless attacks on Jewish communities in Europe throughout the Middle Ages right through the end of World War II.

The lynching in Marion provides a very different theological situation. The white people of Marion were successful in the reassertion of white space through the lynching of two black men. A Girardian analysis of sacrifice shows how the power of lynching these men brought harmony to white space and in turn the white God. Unlike, Tulsa, where the denial of lynching led to widespread religious violence, Marion was an example in which the white community received satisfaction which led to relatively peaceful (do not read just or unpainful) expression of the dominance of white supremacy. The photograph used shows in detail how the people of God joyfully partook in the lynching. A lynching event like the one in Marion should be read as a moment of divine transcendence for the whites involved. Like a revival can lead to the reassurance or empowerment of faith, a lynching event is the theological reaffirmation of one's connection to God and one's own place within white spatiality.

Moving to Detroit, the place of white space is clearer than with either Tulsa or Marion. With legalized segregation, the idea of white space becomes twofold. First is the obvious connection to geographic space. The Federal Housing Authority and the white people of Detroit used segregation to ensure the power and prosperity of white space as opposed to the spaces left for nonwhites. The second piece returns to the place of theological space. With the forced separation of blacks from whites in the E-W area, the federal government and the white people of Detroit seeking to relocate to that geographical space made clear that they saw the proximity of blackness to be a direct threat. The construction of the wall codified this threat by attempting to forcibly keep the two groups of people apart. In trying to ensure separation, whites were performing a ritual act of purification. The blackness at the perceived doorstep of white space was more than a simple inconvenience. The presence of blackness threatened to destroy the bonds of white people with the white God. It was not acceptable for black space to physically touch white space. This would make the construction of the wall more than a political compromise for FHA funding. The wall became a ritual cleanse to ensure there was a barrier between whites and blacks.

The next chapter further explicates the place of the government in maintaining and protecting the white nation. It shows how the concept of white space as sacred to the white God shifted from sacred space to salvific space. The turn moves from acts of violence, either physical or overt, to the sacredness of belonging to the chosen people through the power of citizenship as the only route to membership in the priesthood.

NOTES

1. J.M. Merrill, "Rioting at Tulsa Shames the Nation," (*Detroit Free Press*, June 8, 1921), 6.
2. Ibid.
3. "Rioting Charged to Tulsa Negroes," (*Atlanta Constitution*, June 8, 1921), 9.
4. Chris M. Messer, "The Tulsa Race Riot of 1921: Toward an Integrative Theory of Collective Violence," *Journal of Social History* 44, no. 4(Summer 2011): 1222.
5. Oklahoma Commission to Study the Tulsa Race Riot of 1921, *Tulsa Race Riot*, House Joint Resolution 1035 (1997), February 28, 2001, 58.
6. James H. Cone, *The Cross and the Lynching Tree* (Maryknoll, NY: Orbis Books, 2011), 7.
7. R. Halliburton, Jr., "The Tulsa Race War of 1921," *Journal of Black Studies* 2, no. 3 (March 1972): 336.
8. Ibid.
9. Ibid., 337.
10. Ibid.
11. Ibid., 338.
12. Ibid.
13. Ismail Muhammad, "The 1921 Tulsa Race Riot," *Los Angeles Sentinel* 77, no. 26 (2011).
14. Chris M. Messer and Patricia A. Bell, "Mass Media and Governmental Framing of Riots: The Case of Tulsa, 1921," *Journal of Black Studies* 40, no. 5 (May 2010): 853.
15. Halliburton, Jr., "The Tulsa Race War of 1921," 341.
16. Ibid., 342.
17. "Police Aided Tulsa Rioters: Armed White Ruffians Who Begged for Guns," *Chicago Defender*, June 11, 1921.
18. "Klan Head Asks Tulsa to Rally: Preacher, in Address at 'Riot City,' Defends Ku Klux Klan," *Chicago Defender*, August 20, 1921.
19. The system of "Jewish ghettos" in Nazi Germany was extensive. While the term refers back to the island on which Jews were forced to live in Venice centuries before the Nazi regime, the term "ghetto" persisted during Nazism and afterwards with various connotations. Ghettos were used by Christian communities to separate Jews from the larger society. The Nazi use of ghettos began with the start of World War II in September 1939 and continued in various levels of use for most of the war. Signposts or the construction of walls marked the ghettos. The liquidation of the ghettos began as the Nazi regime instituted the final solution in 1942. Liquidation was carried out in many steps. Jews who left the ghetto on trains headed for either killing fields or death camps like Chełmno were replaced by Jews from other parts of the Greater Reich. The process of removing Jews involved the collection of all Jews selected for deportation and the marching of the selected Jews through the streets of the city to the train station. The Nazi guards forced the Jews onto trains for deportation. This process often included the detaining of the selected Jews in makeshift prisons in order to ensure they could not escape their fate. For more information, see Peter

Hayes and John K Roth, eds., *The Oxford Handbook to Holocaust Studies* (New York: Oxford University Press, 2010) and Doris L. Bergen, *War and Genocide: A Concise History of the Holocaust* (New York: Rowman and Littlefield Publishers, Inc., 2003).

20. Messer and Bell, "Mass Media and Governmental Framing of Riots," 853.

21. "Rioting Charged to Tulsa Negroes," *Atlanta Constitution*, June 8, 1921.

22. Scott Ellsworth, *Death in a Promised Land: The Tulsa Race Riot of 1921* (Baton Rouge: Louisiana State University Press, 1982), 50.

23. René Girard, *Violence and the Sacred*, trans. by Patrick Gregory (Baltimore: John Hopkins University Press, 1977), 15.

24. Paul Tillich, *Theology of Culture*, edited by Robert C. Kimball (New York: Oxford University Press, 1959), 32.

25. "Klan Head Asks Tulsa to Rally: Preacher, in Address at 'Riot City' Defends Ku Klux Principles," *Chicago Defender*, August 20, 1921, 1.

26. Andrew S. Buckser, "Lynching as Ritual in the American South," *Berkeley Journal of Sociology* 37 (1992): 13.

27. James H. Madison, *A Lynching in the Heartland: Race and Memory in America* (New York: Palgrave MacMillan, 2001), 13. Lynching statistics vary widely between sources. While Madison states there were 4,697 lynchings in the U.S., Arthur F. Raper reports 3,724. For an overview of the variants in determining lynching statistics, see Lisa D. Cook, "Converging to a National Lynching Database: Recent Developments" (East Lansing: Michigan State University Department of Economics, 2011). Accessed on March 14, 2015, https://www.msu.edu/~lisacook/hist_meths_lynch_paper_final.pdf.

28. Kelly J. Baker, *Gospel According to the Klan: The KKK's Appeal to Protestant America, 1915–1930* (Lawrence: University Press of Kansas, 2011), 3.

29. Buckser, "Lynching as Ritual in the American South," 13.

30. Angela Sims, "Nooses in Public Spaces: A Womanist Critique of Lynching— A 21st Century Ethical Dilemma," *The Journal of the Society of Christian Ethics* 29, no. 2 (Fall/Winter 2009): 90.

31. Buckser, "Lynching as Ritual in the American South," 11.

32. "5,000 See Mob Hang Rapists in Court Yard," *Chicago Daily Tribune*, August 8, 1930.

33. Ibid., and "Indiana Mob Murders Two; Police Aid K.K.K. Hoodlums," *Chicago Defender*, August 16, 1930.

34. "The President Speaks," *New York Amsterdam News*, August 27, 1930.

35. "Indiana Mob Murders Two".

36. Harvey Young, "The Black Body as Souvenir in American Lynching," *Theatre Journal* 57 (2005): 641.

37. Madison, *A Lynching in the Heartland*, 74.

38. The self-reported religious affiliation of Christians numbered just over 50,000,000 in 1926. See United States Bureau of Census, *Religious Bodies: 1926*, vol. 1 (Washington, D.C.: U.S. Government Printing Office, 1930), 13.

39. Buckser, "Lynching as Ritual in the American South," 20.

40. Arthur F. Raper, *The Tragedy of Lynching* (Chapel Hill: The University of North Carolina Press, 1933), 13.

41. Sims, "Nooses in Public Spaces," 82.

42. Ibid.

43. Raper, *The Tragedy of Lynching*, 80.

44. Ibid., 71.

45. Stephen G. Ray, Jr., "Contending for the Cross: Black Theology and the Ghosts of Modernity," *Black Theology: An International Journal* 8, no. 1 (2010): 54.

46. Raper, *The Tragedy of Lynching*, 54.

47. Angela D. Sims, "The Issue of Race and Lynching," in *Womanist Theological Ethics: A Reader*, edited by Katie Geneva Cannon, Emilie M. Townes, and Angela D. Sims (Louisville: Westminster John Knox Press, 2011), 209.

48. Gregor Ziemer, *Education for Death: The Making of the Nazi* (New York: Oxford University Press, 1941), 17.

49. Sims, "The Issue of Race and Lynching," 212.

50. Donald G. Matthews, "The Southern Rite of Human Sacrifice: Lynching in the American South" *The Mississippi Quarterly* 61, no. 1–2 (Winter–Spring 2008): 56.

51. Ibid.

52. Girard, *Violence and the Sacred*, 14.

53. Matthews, "The Southern Rite of Human Sacrifice," 55.

54. Girard, *Violence and the Sacred*, 79.

55. Mills, *The Racial Contract* (Ithaca, NY: Cornell University Press, 1997), 100.

56. Madison, *A Lynching in the Heartland*, 10.

57. Ibid., 112–3.

58. Ibid., 113.

59. Cone, *The Cross and the Lynching Tree*, 9.

60. Thomas J. Sugrue, *The Origins of the Urban Crisis: Race and Inequality in Postwar Detroit* (Princeton: Princeton University Press, 2005), 19.

61. Ibid., 22.

62. Ta-Nehisi Coates, "The Case for Reparations," *Atlantic*, June 2014, March 3, 2015, http://www.theatlantic.com/features/archive/2014/05/the-case-for-reparations/361631/.

63. Ibid.

64. Thomas J. Sugrue, *The Origins of the Urban Crisis: Race and Inequality in Postwar Detroit* (Princeton: Princeton University Press, 2005), 39.

65. Ibid., 64.

66. Ibid.

67. Burniece Avery, *Walk Quietly Through the Night and Cry Softly* (Detroit: Balamp Publishing, 1977), 147–8.

68. Sugrue, *The Origins of the Urban Crisis,* 64–5.

69. Ibid., 67.

70. Ibid., 69.

71. Ibid., 67.

72. Ibid.

73. Ibid., 68.

74. Marvel Daines, *Be It So Ever Tumbled: The Story of a Suburban Slum* (Citizen's Housing and Planning Council of Detroit, March 1940), 51.

75. Sugrue, *The Origins of the Urban Crisis*, 68.

76. Ibid.
77. Ibid.
78. Ibid., 69.
79. Ibid., 71.
80. Ibid.
81. Ibid., 72.
82. Orlando Patterson, *Slavery and Social Death: A Comparative Study* (Cambridge: Harvard University Press, 1982), 39.

Chapter 5

The Priesthood of All Believers

On a warm July day in 1776, members of the Second Continental Congress read aloud to the gathering crowd in front of the Pennsylvania State House the following: "We hold these truths to be self-evident, that all men are created equal, that they are endowed by their Creator with certain inalienable Rights, that among these are Life, Liberty, and the Pursuit of Happiness." These words are held in the very fabric of the United States' national consciousness and are celebrated across the United States every year on July 4. The founders of the United States sought to free themselves from the British monarchy in order to assure their freedom from an exploitive system; but what did the group of fifty-six white men envision when they signed the Declaration of Independence? Almost 250 years after the first July 4 celebration, the United States is still determining what that famous line of American myth means to the country.

The final step in demonstrating the existence of the religion of white supremacy is to bring together the power of the epistemology of whiteness and the ontology of white supremacy to their natural conclusion in the form of soteriology. The culmination of the religion of white supremacy in the soteriology of white flesh brings together the religious community into a priesthood of all believers. This means that through the salvific power of whiteness a community is born that is predicated on its commonality. This is not just a belief in the sacredness of whiteness. The soteriology of white flesh is the culmination of mind and body coming together in a dynamic way to center ultimacy in the full power of white supremacy in every aspect of culture. In turning to the white Christ to demonstrate the soteriology of white flesh, I am not only suggesting that because the dominant form of Christ in the United States is a white man that there must be a religion of white supremacy. Rather, it is the cultural clinging to the white Christ that makes the turn to the religious necessary. The white Christ symbolizes a much larger cultural system that operates in the United States as a way of regulating the larger society.

In this chapter, the power of the white Christ becomes evident through the consolidation of the religious community. This is done through an analysis of how citizenship is defined from the inception of the United States onward. Through the strict policing of who is a citizen in the United States, a religious community based on white supremacy is born. This priesthood is maintained through the power of law to ensure that the cultural understanding of race is shaped and reshaped to ensure that the soteriological power of citizenship is eternally tied to white flesh. The soteriology of white flesh ensures the power of whites in the nation, but at the same time, it marks those who are not white. This mark is an eternal stamp that defines one as a heathen Other.

In this chapter, I deconstruct three different times in the history of the United States where "all men are created equal" was redefined in more exclusivist terms. Unlike the previous two chapters that demonstrated how various historical events shaped how white supremacist Christianity constrained and used indigenous bodies and blacks, this chapter focuses on how debates over immigration endowed certain people with the privilege of whiteness. The determination of citizenship in the United States has acted as a form of unholy baptism that endows its recipients with privileges contained in the distinction of citizen that increasingly made the ideals of Christian, citizen, and white synonymous. The first part of the chapter looks at the Rule of Naturalization Act of 1790 and how citizenship was defined based on Western motifs of civilized and uncivilized. This builds on the formalization of white space as sacred from previous chapters. One of the first laws passed by the newly formed constitutional government made clear that only white persons could become citizens of the nation. The framers intended to construct the new nation as legalized white space. In building a nation for white people, the idea of white space is expanded not just from the holy interaction of whites with their God but to a more temporal place of legalized white supremacy. The 1790 law formalized the religion of white supremacy as more than a belief system that operated among its followers, as an actual system in which the ultimacy of white supremacy was confirmed in daily interaction through the rule of law.

The second piece of the chapter shifts to the establishment of immigration quotas in the early twentieth century and the debate over the relationship of race and perceived ability for self-governance. This debate hinged on admitting "the right kind of people" into the body politic in order to ensure certain people controlled the country. The court cases of *Ozawa* and *Thind* demonstrate how the rule of law in the United States in terms of race consciousness relied on people within the religious community to ensure the purity of the priesthood. The court's misstep in rationale in *Ozawa* nearly doomed the idea of America as a white nation, but the judges proved the ultimacy of white supremacy in constructing a new interpretation of law completely based on the notions of those within the priesthood. In turn, the idea of citizenship in the white nation became contingent not just on sharing the same physical space or ideals as members of the nation, but also on commonality of white flesh as the primary marker of the priesthood. The presence of white flesh was *sine qua non*.

The final piece transitions to contemporary arguments on immigration from the Americas, particularly on illegal aliens and the passage of Arizona's Senate Bill 1070 in 2010. Like the Black Codes from after the Civil War, the state of Arizona sought to establish a legal system in which merely looking like a suspect made one illegal. It took the idea of white space as sacred and used it as a litmus test for belonging in the white nation. The presence of non-white flesh meant an automatic intrusion on white space. As more nonwhite persons invaded white space, it became important to ensure the ultimacy of white supremacy. These three pieces of legislation demonstrate the ebbs and flow of citizenship status in the United States. What will be apparent in this chapter is the centrality of whiteness to the privileges of citizenship.

A COUNTRY FOR WHITE PEOPLE

Two centuries after the first British colonists arrived on the east coast of North America, their descendants established a new country based on the principles of freedom and liberty. The decades after the ratification of the U.S. Constitution brought many uncertainties to the new republic that the U.S. Congress had to settle. First among these issues to face the nation was the question of naturalization. Who would be considered a citizen of the new country, and more importantly, what were the desired characteristics of future citizens? On March 20, 1790, the U.S. Congress passed the Rule of Naturalization Act establishing the country's initial requirements to become a citizen. The law stated "that any alien, being a free *white*[1] person, who shall have resided within the limits and under the jurisdiction of the United States for a term of two years, may be admitted to become a citizen thereof . . . ."[2] This law established a baseline understanding of naturalization for the next eighty years until the Fourteenth Amendment gave African-American men the right to vote.[3] During these decades, the residency requirements for citizens changed drastically from the initial two years to fourteen years with a declaration renouncing citizenship and other privileges from one's previous country of residence.[4] The country's views on residency changed throughout this time, but one constant was the qualification of whiteness. The definition of white fluctuated in future immigration debates, but with the 1790 law, the matter of importance was the denial of citizenship to black persons in the United States. This included blacks that were indentured, and more importantly, freed blacks.[5] The concept of whiteness was not always foundational in the lived experiences of the former British colonies. In fact, none of the colonial charters of the seventeenth century referred to whites. Instead, the charters focused on dichotomous terms like "civilized" and "uncivilized" to establish authority of the given land.[6] Terms like "heathen," "barbarian," or "savage" were common in describing the indigenous peoples of the Americas and the black bodies brought from West Africa.[7] These concepts were important to understanding the relationship between European settlers and those who lacked Euro-Christian value structures and meanings. The differentiation between civilized and savage began immediately upon the arrival of the Spanish in the Americas, but it took a different meaning as the British applied their notions of civilized and heathen in North America.[8]

This difference is foundational to understanding the perspective and trajectory of race and racism in the history of the United States. To recall from chapter 2, the theological debate between Sepúlveda and las Casas hinged on the way each theological group understood Scripture, and the work of philosophers like Aristotle. Sepúlveda held to an argument that focused on the barbarous nature of the peoples of the Americas, in which Christianity, as a civilizing tool, could be used to teach indigenous peoples to live in appropriate manners.[9] His argument focused on the ways in which the people of the Americas were living. By subjecting themselves to the rule of the Spanish, indigenous peoples could obtain the knowledge and ontological benefits of the Christian faith, as well as the Spanish ideals of right living.[10] Sepúlveda theoretically believed in the ability of the Indian people, while not completely, to adopt the Spanish way of society and culture.

In this construction, the people of the Americas were unenlightened barbarians who, with the help and knowledge of the Spanish, could draw off the cloak of their barbarousness and become acceptable people within the European colonial system and act in God's intended manner for humans. After all, it was understood during the sixteenth century that humans had complete dominion over the Earth and should act as such instead of as one of the many animals that roam the continents.[11]

The way Rebecca Goetz looks at hereditary heathenism in *The Baptism of Early Virginia* is very interesting for the historical ramifications of the establishment of slavery in colonial Virginia, and it demonstrates how the theological underpinnings of Christianity were fluid within the context of the colonies, particularly in relationship to the indigenous and African bodies that did not have inherent rights to the Christian myth. This set up a motif where it became particularly dangerous for the civilized order of Virginia when indentured Africans and indigenous peoples started to claim Christianity for their own through the sacramental act of baptism that theologically shifted the sands of the colonial hierarchy. This was a problem for the colonial project because its initial mission was twofold. First, the colonists sought to civilize and convert non-Europeans. Secondly, European explorers traveled to acquire wealth for their respective empires.[12] The problem with fulfilling both of these missions in the early part of the colonial project, before the baptismal laws that Goetz so eloquently discusses, is that to baptize means to free the baptized or, more importantly for this discussion, to give agency to the colonized person. Agency is key because it is what separates those who are free from those who are not.

The creation of baptism laws in the colonies, like Virginia, which redefined this relationship forever, reinscribed how the theological and social hierarchies operate in the world and enable the colonial project to continue to operate in the supposedly postmodern academy and world. The reason for this is the redefinition of baptism and the meaning of faith and Christianity's connections to freedom in the West, particularly during Western expansion when conversion meant some possible level of freedom. The legal sleight of hand that changed baptism from a hope of earthly freedom to eschatological freedom also created a theological bait and switch that solidified the theological hierarchy that traces back to the philosophy of Aristotle and the theologies of Augustine and Martin Luther.[13]

The theological consequence of separating baptism from freedom made it possible at the very nexus of modern racism to imbed a theological hierarchal racism that places Christians within a divine history wholly separate from paganism, or, by the time of the colonial project, heathens. These non-Christians now had no way socially or theologically of breaking their heathenism due to the unbreakable hierarchy that only presented agency to those who could be trusted with baptism, as the colonial legislatures, with the support of their respective empires, declared Africans and indigenous peoples unworthy of baptism. This declaration subsequently also made manifest a political hierarchy in which Europeans also were not fit for the freedoms that were inherently bestowed in baptism.[14] As a result of these colonial laws that Goetz describes, her concept of hereditary heathenism provides ramifications for the Western theological project.

Sylvester Johnson expounds on the theological significance of heathenism in the United States through his analysis of the myth of Ham from Genesis 9 and how its revelatory influence in the United States helped construct the interweaving of the divine relationship with whiteness. According to Johnson, the use of the Hamitic tradition in the U.S. manifestation of Christianity took on an ontological character of legitimate and illegitimate adherents of the Christian faith.[15] The myth is based on a particular reading of Genesis

9:18–28 that establishes Africans as the descendants of Ham. This means that Noah's curse that all of Ham's descendants would be slaves gave justification to enslaving Africans.[16] Through this interpretation, the ontological significance of blackness defined the bearer of the black distinction regardless of one's conversion to Christianity. In the tradition of white supremacist Christianity, religious affiliation mattered little in the outlook of one's destiny. To be black meant always to be black. This was possible because of the American connection to the Bible. Johnson argues that the Bible represents much more than a way of making sense of the world.[17] The Bible was a meaning-making symbol of white supremacist Christianity. Adherents to white Christianity viewed themselves as actually participating in the narrative of Scripture, and delineation of the Hamitic myth made it impossible to reconcile the ontic state of blackness as established by the Curse of Ham with adherence to the Christian faith. Regardless of Christian conversion, the power of the myth destined those who were affected by the curse to an eternal status of illegitimate.[18]

The nineteenth-century version of white supremacist Christianity understood the world through the lens of religious identification. This meant that while blacks, even Christian blacks, were stained by illegitimacy due to their ontological distinction as illegitimate, whites took on a radically different form of identity. For white supremacist Christianity, it meant that God ordained whites as the purveyors of the American nation.[19] The chosenness of white flesh transformed the religiosity of Christianity in the United States into an imperialistic god. The ultimacy of whiteness in the meaning of the Christian tradition as experienced in the United States altered the ability of the faith to be practiced without the total commitment of its followers to the eradication of heathenism. In this way, Johnson demonstrates the shift of Christ from a suffering savior to a conqueror of heathenism.[20] The conquering Christ gave the power of ultimate meaning to the adherents of white supremacist Christianity with an identity as a people.

This was not a symbolic relationality like the pride of country; rather, as Johnson argues, the identity white Christianity attaches to is the insidiousness of the German term *Volk*.[21] The symbolism of *das Volk* is not found in the standard definition of the word as a people. *Volk* connects to an idea of a certain group of people who find meaning in a common set of symbols and belief in the power of their commonality. As such, *das Volk* is most commonly understood through the articulation of the Nazi form of nationalism. The Nazi system of meaning created a correlation between national identity and the framing of a particular set of racial ideals.[22] By the time of the rise of Nazism as the governing party in Germany in 1933, the connection of a people (as the standard definition of *Volk* asserts) was transformed into an amalgamation of a particular group of people in their relationship to the concept of Germanness.[23] This interweaving of racial coding with national identity set up a system of meaning that based ultimacy in a particular understanding of *Volk*. Nazi Germany turned the power of space into an ultimate concern that established an "against-each-otherness" as manifested through racial imperialism.

Goetz and Johnson's explications on heathenism point to the same sort of operation that took place in North America. The construction of the American identity in relationship to the myths and symbolism of Christianity created an American *Volk*. The theological framing of divine affiliation as opposed to heathenism was not one of simple adherence to the Christian faith. By the mid-nineteenth century, white supremacist Christianity had developed its own notion of space that found ultimate meaning not in the messianic symbolism of Christ on the cross, but rather in the power of white identity.[24] The ultimacy of white supremacist Christianity did not take shape exclusively as a nineteenth-century phenomenon. The process of constructing the divinity of whiteness took centuries, and each particular step built upon the last.

The notion of hereditary heathenism was furthered played out in the passage of the Rule of Naturalization Act of 1790. The legislators of the new country used the term "white" as a coded way to determine who was fit and unfit for the burdens of freedom and liberty that the new republic bestowed on all eligible men.[25] The late eighteenth-century thinkers in the United States viewed the concepts of civilization and whiteness as synonymous with each other. This is proven by the floor debates prior to the passage of the 1790 act. As Matthew Frye Jacobson argues, the discussion over the merits of the law was not the efficacy of whiteness; rather, the legislators wondered if they made it too easy for other whites to receive citizenship.

> So natural was the relationship of whiteness to citizenship that, in the debate which followed, the racial dimension of the act remained unquestioned. Members of the first Congress argued over the one year requirement (should it have been two or three?); they wondered whether Jews and Catholics should be eligible; they entertained a proposal for a period of political "probation" for newcomers and pondered limitations on the right to hold political office; they argued over foreigners' rights of land-holding and inheritance; they worried about the potential threat posed by "monarchists," former "nobles," and criminals from other lands. They debated the naturalization process and wondered whether they had made citizenship "much too easy" to attain—should claimants be required, for example, to provide witnesses to their good character? In general the nation's first legislators saw the law as too inclusive rather than too exclusive, and nowhere did they pause to question the limitation of naturalized citizenship to "white persons."[26]

The inclusion of "free white person" makes a clear delineation in the rights of citizenship as framed by the First Congress. They established, from the outset, a racial caste system that not only asserted but also carried the weight of God's ordination, that only a certain type of person deserved the freedoms the new republic offered. Since the establishment of the "white person" classification in 1790 to the passage of the Immigration and Nationality Act of 1965, immigration in the United States has hinged on the interpretation of these two words. Before the ratification of the Fourteenth Amendment, the addition of "free" clearly held significant meaning in the determination of eligibility for citizenship, but even with the passage of the amendment, debates over citizenship qualifications continued.

MAKING THE WHITE CHRIST THE LAW OF THE LAND

Subsequent generations of American citizens and those who desired to be citizens continued to debate the meaning of "free white persons." Half a century after the ratification of the Fourteenth Amendment, the status of immigrants became particularly important. As a way to fill the void in the legal framework of naturalization, the Supreme Court of the United States (SCOTUS) used judicial legislating to solidify "white person" as essential to citizenship. The cases of Takao Ozawa in 1922 and Bhagat Singh Thind in 1923 epitomized the power of the fluidity of whiteness to ensure the centralization of power within a certain subsection of the U.S. populations, namely those of Western Europe with an affinity toward Christian Protestantism.[27] As will become clear through the analysis of the *Ozawa* and *Thind* cases, the SCOTUS created legal precedent for the denial of naturalization to Asians based on a legally produced status of racial unsuitability for citizenship.[28]

In 1894, Takao Ozawa arrived in San Francisco from Japan at the age of nineteen. During his time in California, Ozawa graduated from high school and attended the University of California, Berkeley.[29] In 1906, Ozawa left the San Francisco area for the Territory of Hawaii, where he would spend the rest of his life.[30] On October 16, 1914, Ozawa sought to formalize his residency in the United States by applying for naturalization in the U.S. District Court for the Territory of Hawaii.[31] The U.S. district attorney for Hawaii opposed Ozawa's petition, and the District Court denied the petition because of Ozawa's classification as a member of the Japanese race; he was ineligible for naturalization due to the "free white persons" clause.[32] Ozawa appealed to the Ninth Circuit of Appeals, which sent the case to SCOTUS. Ozawa argued that he should be granted naturalization based on his ability to assimilate to American culture and a proper reading of the framers' intent in the passage of the Naturalization Act of 1790. Devon W. Carbado states the argument this way: "Ozawa argued that the 1790 naturalization statute did not rely on a racial classification scheme. The term 'free white person' was 'used simply to distinguish black people from others.' For Ozawa, slavery was a normative racial baseline; the naturalization statute did no more than reflect this baseline and did not establish new racial classifications."[33] In essence, Ozawa argued for understanding the 1790 statute as a way to make enslaved blacks ineligible for citizenship while providing the opportunity to everyone else who met the other requirements. His argument was founded on the belief of a strict black/white dichotomy rather than one that considered further racial classification. This meant that blacks were ineligible while everyone else had the right to citizenship. This line of thinking would mean that when blacks received the privileges of citizenship in 1870 that naturalization was available to everyone regardless of racial differences.

When Ozawa's case reached SCOTUS, a drastically different approach would be applied to the 1790 statute. *Takao Ozawa v. United States* (260 U.S. 178) was argued before the court on October 3–4, 1922.[34] The case was decided five weeks later on November 13, 1922, with the court ruling unanimously that Ozawa was ineligible for naturalization because he was a member of the Japanese race and therefore not a "free white person."[35] Associate Justice George Sutherland wrote the opinion of the court. From the beginning, Sutherland conceded that Ozawa "was well qualified by character and education for citizenship."[36] While conceding that based on individual merits Ozawa was qualified for naturalization, he argued that this was not the most important modicum for citizenship.

After admitting Ozawa's personal merits, Sutherland used the remainder of his brief opinion to state bluntly that Japanese people were not white. In referring to the 1790 statute, Associate Justice Sutherland stated:

> The intention was to confer the privilege of citizenship upon that class of persons whom the fathers knew as white, and to deny it to all who could not be so classified. It is not enough to say that the framers did not have in mind the brown or yellow races of Asia. It is necessary to go farther and be able to say that had these particular races been suggested the language of the act would have been so varied as to include them within its privileges.[37]

Sutherland's use of the *argumentum ex silento* fallacy rejected Ozawa's claim that a strict dichotomy of black and white would make him eligible for naturalization. To continue his line of argument, Justice Sutherland extrapolated the meaning of "white person" in this way:

> The determination that the words "white person" are synonymous with the words "a person of the Caucasian race" simplifies the problem, although it does not entirely dispose of it. Controversies have ere arisen and will no doubt arise again in respect to the proper classification of individuals in border line cases. The effect of the conclusion that the words "white person" mean Caucasian is

not to establish a sharp line of demarcation between those who are entitled and those who are not entitled to naturalization, but rather a zone of more or less debatable ground outside of which, upon the one hand are those clearly ineligible for citizenship. Individual cases falling within this zone must be determined as they arise from time to time by what this Court has called, in another connection, "the gradual process of judicial inclusion and exclusion."[38]

On this basis, SCOTUS ruled that Ozawa, as a member of the Japanese race, was clearly outside the scope of those who were considered Caucasian and subsequently ineligible for citizenship. This peculiar paragraph from Justice Sutherland's opinion is all the more important because it established a judicial precedence that would be influential in the *Thind* case. As for the *Takao Ozawa* case, SCOTUS used the merits of scientific inquiry to prove (in their mind) the indisputable connection between the framers' use of "white person" in 1790 and the modern scientific classification of Caucasian. This clearly made it impossible for any immigrant not classified as Caucasian to receive the oft-wanted status of American citizen.

Four months after SCOTUS ruled against Ozawa, it had the chance to further solidify its interpretation of "white person" as it pertains to one's eligibility for naturalization. In 1913, a Sikh named Bhagat Singh Thind arrived in the United States from the Punjab region of British-controlled India.[39] He came to the United States as a student and would later serve in the U.S. military during World War I. Thind was discharged from the military in 1918, and two years later, he decided to make his commitment to the U.S. official by applying for naturalization. The District Court of Oregon heard his case where, like the *Ozawa* case, the district attorney opposed the petition for naturalization.[40] Unlike the *Ozawa* case, the District Court of Oregon granted Mr. Thind a certificate of citizenship and later affirmed this decision when the United States filed an appeal stating that the applicant was not a white person and therefore ineligible for naturalization.[41] The United States appealed the decision to the Circuit Court of Appeals for the Ninth Circuit. The Circuit Court of Appeals sent the case to SCOTUS. The only reason the case reached SCOTUS is that the United States pursued this case to ensure that Thind's certificate of naturalization was not confirmed.[42]

SCOTUS agreed to hear the case on January 11–12, 1923, and rendered their decision on February 19, 1923. Thind's counsel argued that Thind qualified as Caucasian due to his Aryan ancestry. By using the rationale of the opinion of the court in *Ozawa v. United States*, Thind could reasonably expect his previously granted certificate of naturalization to be upheld by SCOTUS. This was not the case. In another unanimous decision, the court ruled against Thind on the basis that he was not a white person.[43] As with the *Ozawa* case, Associate Justice Sutherland authored the opinion of the court in which the court's opinion would be determinative in immigration regulations for decades.

Once again, Justice Sutherland started his argument by stating that Mr. Thind's individual merits were worthy of naturalization, but that these accomplishments had no bearing on who was and who was not eligible for citizenship.[44] While Sutherland clearly stated that Thind's personal qualifications were not in question, he quickly turned to laying out an argument for Thind's unsuitability for American citizenship. In light of the court's ruling in *Ozawa v. United States*, Thind's counsel focused on his connection to the clause "white person" because of his people's classification as Caucasian. Based on Sutherland's opinion in the Ozawa case, Thind's naturalization should have never been questioned, but when the ruling was released, SCOTUS's rationale for determining "white person" had radically changed.

The court sought to discredit Thind's certificate of naturalization by deconstructing his claims to citizenship by claiming membership in the Caucasian race based on popular conjecture. Sutherland began by stating:

> Mere ability on the part of an applicant for naturalization to establish a line of descent from a Caucasian ancestor will not *ipso facto* and necessarily conclude the inquiry. "Caucasian" is a conventional word of much flexibility, as a study of literature dealing with racial questions will disclose, and while it and the words "white person" are treated as synonymous for the purposes of that case, they are not of identical meaning—*idem per idem.*[45]

According to Sutherland, Thind's case did not warrant an open and shut interpretation based on the application of Sutherland's own words from four months earlier in *Ozawa v. United States* that "white person" simply meant Caucasian.

In a new interpretation of his own opinion in Ozawa, Justice Sutherland went further to state that a common understanding of the framers' use of "white person" must be applied in cases that fall inside the zone of judicial interpretation:

> In the endeavor to ascertain the meaning of the statute we must not fail to keep in mind that it does not employ the word "Caucasian" but the words "white persons," and these are words of common speech and not of scientific origin. The word "Caucasian" not only was not employed in the law but was probably wholly unfamiliar to the original framers of the statute in 1790 . . . It is in the popular sense of the word, therefore, that we employ it as an aid to the construction of the statute, for it would be obviously illogical to convert words of common speech used in a statute into words of scientific terminology when neither the latter nor the science for whose purposes they were coined was within the contemplation of the framers of the statute or of the people for whom it was framed.[46]

Justice Sutherland continued his argument by stating:

> They imply, as we have said, a racial test; but the term "race" is one which, for
> the practical purposes of the statute, must be applied to a group of living persons
> now possessing in common requisite characteristics, not to groups of persons,
> who are supposed to be or really are descended from some remote, common
> ancestor but who, whether they both resemble to a greater or less extent, have,
> at any rate, ceased altogether to resemble one another. It may be true that the
> blond Scandinavian and the brown Hindu have a common ancestor in the dim
> reaches of antiquity, but the average man knows perfectly well that there are
> unmistakable and profound differences between them today . . . In 1790 the
> Adamite theory of creation—which gave common ancestor to all mankind—
> was generally accepted, and it is not at all probable that it was intended by the
> legislators of that day to submit the question of the application of the words
> "white person" to the mere test of an indefinitely common ancestry, without
> regards to the subsequent divergence of the various branches from such com-
> mon ancestry or from one another.[47]

The crux of U.S. immigration policy is found in these words authored by
Associate Justice George Sutherland. The essence of "white person" meant
that only persons like those who "founded" this country are eligible for
citizenship. This framework for American citizenship harkens to Rebecca
Goetz's concept of hereditary heathenism that she applied to the formation
of the slave class in colonial Virginia and how it relates to the Naturalization
Act of 1790; yet, 130 years after the framers conceived of a land for "free
white persons," the government of the United States continued to follow the
theological demarcation of Christian and heathen. The difference here is the
language used to justify hereditary heathenism in the first half of the twentieth
century. In both the *Ozawa* and *Thind* cases, SCOTUS advanced a theological hierarchy where particular white bodies were endowed with the divine
prerogative of taming creation and in order to fulfill this sacred duty, the community must remain pure. In this way, SCOTUS used science to ensure that
those who were clearly of the heathen caste did not infiltrate the gene pool of
democracy, and in an odd twist, switched its logic to void Thind's citizenship
status to ensure that those who were of mixed race did not grasp the power of
belonging. This thinking applies not only to those who requested naturalization, but also to the future descendants of Thind.

> What we now hold is that the words "free white person" are words of common
> speech, to be interpreted in accordance with the understanding of the common
> man, synonymous with the word "Caucasian" only as that word is popularly
> understood . . . It is a matter of familiar observation and knowledge that the phys-
> ical group characteristics of the Hindus render them readily distinguishable from
> the various groups of persons in this country commonly recognized as white.

The children of English, French, German, Italian, Scandinavian, and other Europe parentage, quickly merge into the mass of our population and those distinctive hallmarks of their European origin. On the other hand, it cannot be doubted that the children born in this country of Hindu parents would retain indefinitely the clear evidence of their ancestry. It is very far from our thought to suggest the slightest question of racial superiority or inferiority. What we suggest is merely racial difference, and it is of such character and extent that the great body of our people instinctively recognize it and reject the thought of assimilation.[48]

Ironically, while Sutherland states that the court is not "suggesting" inferiority or superiority, the judicial opinion is enumerating exactly that distinction. The court's reasoning for denying Thind's claim to citizenship is that he is not European and therefore incapable of assimilating to American culture, whereas European immigrants, with time, could become good American citizens. This means that the main qualification for citizenship is the ability to become "American," but what does this mean? Obviously, Thind's physical features could have been a part of the court's rationale, but Europeans had different racialized characteristics. Ultimately, the court's decision to revoke Thind's citizenship was based primarily on his classification as Hindu.[49] By framing Thind as Hindu, Justice Sutherland was making an important distinction on the idea of citizenship. Sutherland had adopted an ontological understanding of Christianity as it pertained to what it meant to be a U.S. citizen. In Thind's case, Sutherland conceded that science might affirm Thind's citizenship status. This meant that a deeper understanding of citizen based on the combination of Christianity and whiteness was necessary to be worthy of citizenship.

In constructing Thind as Hindu, Justice Sutherland made a theological statement about the place of whiteness in America. This is where it is imperative to return to the importance of the soteriology of white flesh. By framing Thind as eternally other, the citizenship in the priesthood was reaffirmed by ensuring the continued likeness of Christ. This was possible because of Sutherland's insistence of the combination of Christianity and whiteness as corequirements for the status of citizen. Whether Sutherland understood his thinking or not, his decision made the claim that to be truly a citizen meant to be white and vice versa.

Anthony Pinn argues that Sallman's *Head of Christ* represents this constant measure even in the moments when the Christ image is most fluid because its whiteness is not questioned.[50] By this right, groups could move in and out of the accepted race, but the color of Christ reminded people of the common look of white skin that Thind could never possess. Pinn states:

If not an accurate depiction of the physical "look" of the dominant voices and figures of this age, images of Christ—such as Warner Sallman's *The Head of*

Christ—presented Christ constant with an idyllic or iconic image in line with the preferences of many within that age. There are ways in which depictions of Christ—visual images of Jesus Christ—promoted a particular social cohesiveness and sense of collective identity on the cultural-political level. Yet, such images promoted more than a sociopolitical imaginary in that they also spoke to the proper "look" of a citizen, the racially visible markers of belonging. In this regard, one can stretch out the chronology of Christ imaginary by which the meaning of the nineteenth-century hymn, "More Like Jesus," involves a type of normative gaze whereby the indwelling of Christ ethically arranged is deeply associated with the embodied body.[51]

Pinn is pointing to the importance of white supremacy as an age to age constant. While *Head of Christ* was produced after the Supreme Court heard the *Ozawa* and *Thind* cases, Sallman merely painted the cultural truth of the United States. The Christ of Sallman's painting was cultural representation of the place white supremacy holds in U.S. culture and, thus, why it was inconceivable for Justice Sutherland to fathom Thind or his progenitors ever being equal to the measure for the requirement of citizen. Thind's dark skin, classification as Hindu, and turban were incongruent with God's chosen people.

To accept Thind into the priesthood would be heretical to the white God. The problem was not that Thind was in the United States—many nonwhite persons lived in America—it was the idea that citizenship is a type of space. This space is only for those who meet the necessary requirements that the white Christ represents to that age. By ensuring that the priesthood matches the ideals of whiteness at the time, the body of Christ (the people of god) could remain pure within itself. The assurance of having an unparalleled connection as god's people also meant that in times of trial, for example nonwhites seeking the rights of whites, the people of god could stand together for the protection of their Christ.

The god of space is determinative in the construction of the American *Volk*. In establishing who is and who is not eligible for membership in America, white supremacist Christianity is safeguarding the community of believers from possible threats to the god of white supremacy. The delineation established by Justice Sutherland shows that Tillich's idea of "special soil" in the guise of white supremacist Christianity is not only the dirt upon which the United States stakes its claim.[52] The special soil in white supremacist Christianity is held is the embodiment of a particular meaning and value structure centered on the power of whiteness. The unholy baptism that is bestowed upon coreligionists calls each member to protect the community by ensuring the purity of the assembled. Unlike Tillich's construction of space as "beside-each-otherness," this form of space has morphed into an "against-each-otherness" precisely because of the ultimacy found in the symbols and myths surrounding the power of whiteness.[53] This meant in the case of Thind that it was inconceivable to consider him as anything other than an outsider to the community of believers. His impurity made it impossible to accept him as a citizen of the United States because his characteristics were an affront to the god of white supremacy.

The construction of Thind as impure or incapable of citizenship used a particular understanding of the law as interpreted by Justice Sutherland. Ian Haney López argues that in making the decision against Thind, the court used a "common knowledge" approach that placed all reasoning on the account of race in what the justices believed.[54] While the court relied on the connection of white and Caucasian to discount scientific skin tests, this idea could not work when applied to Thind. The country would not accept that the simple connection of white Caucasian could ever make a Hindu white: "For the Court, science fell from grace not when it erroneously confirmed racial differences as in *Ozawa*, but when it contradicted popular prejudice as in *Thind*. These holdings evince that the Court was committed to socially supposed races and racial hierarchies not to search for subtler truths."[55] What the court confronted in Thind was the power of white supremacy. The religion of white supremacy caused a crisis of consciousness among the court. How could they at the same time declare white and Caucasian equal terms, and yet, also say a Sikh was not eligible under the whiteness clause to be a citizen? As Pinn argues, the rationale for race hinges on the belief that God favors white people.[56] There is no way the rationale of white supremacy could grant the status of citizen to a person blatantly antithetical to the divine imaginary.

To this point, Haney López says that "racial categories exist *only* as a function of what people believe."[57] In this instance, the precedent of *Ozawa* became subservient to the beliefs of the court. The law was secondary to religion. The court had to firmly stand for the common knowledge prejudice or contradict their own understanding of their place in the world, and in turn, their relationship with God. It is important to note that the court's crisis was not their own. Congress assured that the question of citizenship was settled the year after *Thind*.[58] To ensure the ultimacy of whiteness, Congress used the lesson of *Thind* to legislate new and strict immigration quotas to ensure people from nonwhite places of the world could not overrun the white city on a hill. The Immigration Act of 1924 would not be overturned until the passage of the Immigration and Nationality Act of 1965.

To be once Hindu meant to never be fully American, and to be fully American meant never to be Hindu, much in the same way that Christianity and heathen took ontic characteristics during the colonization of the Americas. What this shows is the importance of the performance of whiteness in the American psyche. The term White Anglo-Saxon Protestant (WASP) takes on a new dimension when considered in light of SCOTUS's use of the concept of "white person" to limit one's ability to acquire citizenship.[59] While both

Ozawa and Thind had met the performance markers of the American work ethic myth, they did not meet the performative necessities that indelibly mark one as either suitable or not. Again, this is where the religio-cultural convention of Protestant Christianity signifies true citizenship against contingent citizenship. While Ozawa was denied because he was Japanese, Thind's crime was not being biologically Christian, let alone religiously Christian.[60] Biological Christianity points to the ontic nature of Christianity by birthright. Without biological Christianity marked by the WASP designation, one could never receive the socially constructed "wages of whiteness."[61]

ARIZONA AND THE CONSTRUCTION OF BROWN CODES

A century after the SCOTUS used its powers enumerated in Article III of the U.S. Constitution to construct a narrow vision of "white person" as it pertains to qualifications for citizenship, the state of Arizona sought to reignite these conversations through the passage of legislation that redefined the relationship between the state and those residing within its borders. The passage of Senate Bill 1070 manifested legal procedures for the subjugation of the so-called illegal aliens in a state that sits on the international border with Mexico, and therefore finds issues surrounding immigration more poignant in day-to-day life than does the rest of the country. The statutes established for the protection of Arizona citizens seek to provide assistance to law enforcement in order to prevent instances like the murder of Robert Krentz weeks before the passage of the law. While some might think that Arizona's attempt to make the state safer for its legal inhabitants is admirable, such a view fails to account for the unintended consequences of hyper-enforcement of immigration legislation. Is there legal precedent for establishing an illegal class of inhabitants? More importantly, what could be the underlying and pernicious intentions of creating a class status that lies outside the shadow of the U.S. Bill of Rights? In truth, one does not have to strain to find examples similar to SB 1070 in U.S. history. For the purpose of this comparison, I demonstrate the derogatory connections between the passage of SB 1070 in 2010 and the establishment of the infamous Black Codes in southern states in the immediate aftermath of the Civil War.

In the months following the end of Civil War, southern states realized their cultural realities before the war would be nearly impossible to replicate. If the north had their druthers, the institution of chattel slavery would cease, and former slaves, who in their minds lacked the status of fully human, would be forced on southerners, slave owners or not, as supposed equals. In response to this possibility, states passed legislation to limit the freedoms of blacks within former slave states in order to avoid the embarrassing reality of becoming equals with former chattel. The first state to pass these new regulations limiting black life was Mississippi. In November 1865, a mere seven months after the war concluded, the state of Mississippi passed the first set of Black Codes to reestablish the legal precedence for institutionalized white supremacy.[62] This legislation was broad in its approach and, in effect, made any black actions that were not approved by the white power structure illegal. From the outset, the new legislature in Mississippi sought ways to maintain its old power dynamics. This was established through statutes establishing an apprenticeship system, laws against vagrancy, a set of black-only civil rights, and a penal system that was disproportionately harsh on freedpersons who were still minors. In this law, the state legislature ordered local authorities to report to the state "all freedmen, free Negroes, and mulattoes" under the age of eighteen whose parents were not capable or willing to properly support their children.[63] These reports were to be done semiannually, and it was the job of the probate court to find someone to support the allegedly abandoned minors. The particularly atrocious part of this setup was the apprentice concept, wherein the goal of the system was to set up a new form of state-sponsored involuntary servitude of minors. The court would seek to place these black minors with their former masters where the minors were indentured until a certain age.[64]

This program was completely based on the old chattel slavery model in that these "apprentices" were formally bonded to their masters, and the masters were considered their parents who could punish through any means. In addition to becoming the legal parent of an apprentice, the master had complete rights to the body of their apprentice, including legal recourse if the apprentice decided to leave this legal relationship. In the vein of the fugitive slave laws that date back to 1793 which established legal rights of slave owners to seek the return of their property, these new masters could request the state to apprehend their apprentices who left without permission.[65] In addition to this, like the former fugitive slave laws, strict laws were established against whites who aided and abetted these fugitive apprentices. In effect, this apprentice law established legal slavery without the chattel signification, but this law could even apply to nominations through the arbitrary discretion of a judge. The particular piece of importance is how the black body in Mississippi after the war lived in this proverbial state of exception where the federal government established former slaves as having protections under the law, yet agents of this law in some states could arbitrarily indenture persons because of their lack of status as a black body with unenforceable and theoretical rights.

The apprentice laws applied to those whom the state deemed minors, but what about those who had reached an age where the state could not force them to a master? To deal with them, the state of Mississippi established strict vagrancy laws which bore a striking resemblance to SB 1070. In this set of regulations, the state constructed a system wherein the black body was completely regulated by the government. As a part of this law, all freedpersons were required to prove their employment to the local authorities, and failure to prove employment would result in a fine of $150 and a possible ten days in jail.[66] The combination of the fine and jail sentence resulted in an extra layer of punishment for a freedperson deemed a vagrant. The law also stated that failure to pay the fine within five days would result in the freedperson being sold to a white person who paid the fine.[67] The white person could in turn require the freedperson to work off the debt, but this would be nearly impossible because the white master could deduct the cost of housing, food, and clothing from the freedperson's earnings, much in the same way that sharecroppers continually remained in debt to white farmers under Jim Crow.[68]

In addition to the state of Mississippi establishing a new form of slavery, the state constructed provisions that were increasingly harsh for whites that associated with vagrant blacks. Along with this, the state set up an additional tax to be paid only by blacks.[69] This was established to force blacks to pay for the cost of apprehending vagrants and maintaining the courts as a result of these arrests, but another benefit of the tax was the creation of another way to indenture freedpersons. The failure to pay the tax would result in the sale of the freedperson to a white person who paid the tax under the same terms as one's failure to pay the fines for vagrancy and other offences.[70]

To make matters worse for the freedpersons of Mississippi, they also constructed a separate set of civil rights for blacks with a different set of penal codes. The state made clear its desire for whites to control black life by ensuring through law that blacks who desired to own or rent land must do so in incorporated areas.[71] By restricting black residents to incorporated areas, the state of Mississippi placed all blacks with any sort of status or financial influence under the control of white civil officers. Subsequently, this allowed the state to monitor the members of black society that had the most potential to disrupt the status quo. In addition to this, the state instituted miscegenation laws.[72] This granted freedpersons the right to marry (which was new in many slave states), but only to other persons from their race, in order to ensure that whiteness was not defiled by the hazards of blackness.

To compound the statutes enumerated in the vagrancy section, the civil rights of freedpersons were connected to their ability to obtain housing and employment. Mississippi required all freedpersons over the age of eighteen to provide proof of housing and employment yearly. To not provide proof would result in fines and jail terms that were designed to force freedpersons into indentured servitude. Statutes requiring housing and employment were particularly hard for freedpersons to comply with because of the Black Codes' purposeful desire to place blacks beyond the pale of society. The essential example of this deleterious law was the forbidding of employers to hire freedpersons to contracts longer than thirty days without the permission of the courts.[73] This forced freedpersons to be completely reliant on white employers to ensure that they did not enter the no man's land of vagrancy and eventual indentured service. To compound this, it was illegal for blacks to seek employment while under contract with another white employer, and yet, it was illegal to not have a job, so in reality, freedpersons were enslaved whether it was legal or not because they could never leave the service of a white person without risking the death knell of their supposed freedom through the selling of their rights due to vagrancy. The Black Code system was so concrete that a white person could not approach a black person who was under contract to another white person for an employment opportunity.[74] The penalty for such an act was up to a $1,500 fine and six months in jail.[75] The absoluteness of black servitude was even further ensured to their white employer by a clause that privileged the testimony of whites that if they attested that a black person abandoned their contract, the said black person would forfeit their salary for the year and would be sent to jail at their own expense.[76] This humiliation would be complete if the white accuser paid the expense of the black person's jailing, and in turn, the white person would own the rights of the black person until the debt was paid as determined by the white owner. This meant that to seek employment could result in a white person accusing their black employee of abandoning their job, and in turn, the white person acquires the services of the black person indefinitely.

The penal codes further limited the rights of freedpersons by curtailing their access to a sustainable life. The state declared that it was illegal for any freedperson to be in possession of any firearms, ammunition, or deadly weapon.[77] To be caught with such items would result in a $10 fine, the cost of the court proceeding, and forfeiture of all contraband to the person who notified authorities.[78] The only exceptions to this clause were for U.S. military or local officials. The state went further by declaring the following:

> Any freedman, free Negro, or mulatto committing riots, routs, affrays, tres-
> passes, malicious mischief, cruel treatments to animals, seditious speeches,
> insulting gestures, language, or acts, or assaults on any person, disturbance of
> the peace, exercising the function of a minister of the Gospel without a license
> from some regularly organized church, vending spirituous or intoxicating
> liquors, or committing any other misdemeanor . . . be fined not less than $10
> and not more than $100, and may be imprisoned, at the discretion of the court,
> not exceeding thirty days.[79]

In essence, the state of Mississippi made it illegal for freedpersons to do or say anything that might be found suspicious to a white person. To go further, the state, in order to further control black bodies, reinstated all punishments used during chattel slavery.

These various codes established by the state of Mississippi sought to ensure through legal status the superiority of white life by forcing blacks to be completely dependent on whites to ensure they stayed within the biopolitical order, because to be forced outside of this put blacks in a state of exception where they lost complete control of their agency to the white power structure. To be black in Mississippi meant that their being was nothing more than a disposable item of white materiality. If one yielded completely to the white power structure, a freedperson could retain a piece of their human agency, but to commit an affront to whiteness shattered this morsel of agency for a time not limited to the destruction of physical being.

While the Black Codes were eventually abolished, the premise of vagrancy was never fully removed from the legislative possibilities available to states. This distinction became clear in Arizona in response to the death of an American citizen near the Mexican border. On April 23, 2010, Arizona Governor Jan Brewer signed The Support Our Law Enforcement and Safe Neighborhoods Act and immediately sparked a national debate on the role of states in immigration enforcement.[80] The law, better known as Senate Bill 1070 or SB 1070, added a new layer to the long-standing partisan argument over the status of the so-called illegal aliens in the United States. The law itself has a short but powerful impetus that led the state to action on an issue that the check and balances of the U.S. Constitution implies is a federal affair. On March 27, 2010, an Arizona rancher near the border of Mexico was murdered while patrolling his land.[81] The police report stated that in the minutes before his murder, Robert Krentz was on his cellular phone and reported sighting a suspected illegal immigrant who needed assistance.[82] The police believed the suspect had crossed the U.S./Mexico border and murdered Krentz. While there were different theories discussed by local authorities and local and national media in the days that followed, the most prominent theory argued that Krentz was murdered in retribution for a drug raid that had occurred on his property the previous day.

In response to the death of Krentz, a prominent rancher in Arizona who was outspoken on immigration issues, the state legislature passed SB 1070 with the purpose of protecting Arizona residents from the perceived increase in danger along the U.S./Mexico border. The idea of seeking to protect your residents, those who elected the state officials to protect them, is admirable, but how did the legislature and the governor seek to enforce these new protections? The passage of SB 1070 set a new precedent in state enforcement of federal immigration policy by establishing a new legal order that declared anyone who could be an illegal immigrant a threat to the residents of Arizona. The law establishes this belief from the outset:

> The legislature finds that there is a compelling interest in the cooperative enforcement of federal immigration laws throughout all of Arizona. The

legislature declares that the intent of this act is to make attrition though enforcement the public policy of all state and local government agencies in Arizona. The provisions of this act are intended to work together to discourage and deter the unlawful entry and presence of aliens and economic activity of persons unlawfully present in the United States.[83]

Based on the opening paragraph to SB 1070, the legislature is seeking to formalize a caste system within the state of Arizona that places anyone with the designation "illegal" beyond the pale of basic rights as a person residing in the United States. The dichotomy of legal and illegal does not stop with the drive to eliminate those whom the government classifies as not belonging. SB 1070 is the systematic application of legislation to segregate and eliminate from society those that the power structure deems unworthy of life in the context of the United States.

SB 1070 is constructed in such a way that it regulates everything from compulsory enforcement of the law down to the very movement of those who are perceived or suspected to be illegal immigrants. The law states that "for any lawful contact made by a law enforcement official or agency of this state or a country, city, town or other political subdivision of this state where reasonable suspicion exists that the person is an alien who unlawfully present in the United States, a reasonable attempt shall be made, when practicable, to determine the immigration status of the person."[84] This statute establishes the inherent presumed guilt of any person suspected of being an illegal immigrant, but how does one ascertain probable cause? SB 1070 at its foundational level calls into question the legality of being Latina/o in the state of Arizona.

To advance the ontic illegality of Latina/o bodies in Arizona, the state instituted systems of repression and monitoring that do not include provisions for ensuring due process and active measures to prevent racial profiling. In addition to mandating enforcement by all government agents, the state also established a database on all persons suspected of being an illegal immigrant. It declared all illegal immigrants to be trespassing if they enter Arizona and made it illegal to harbor or encourage undocumented workers to reside in Arizona, to provide transportation, to hire undocumented day laborers, or to attempt to aid anyone attempting to cross the U.S./ Mexico border.[85] All crimes laid out in SB 1070 incur significant fines and/or jail sentences for both illegal immigrants and those convicted of aiding them in any way. The law is particularly insidious in its prosecution of illegal immigrants. Statute 13–1509c states that when it is determined that one is in the country illegally, they must pay the fine and serve the full jail sentence before Arizona will transfer the person to U.S. Department of Homeland Security for deportation. Another element to this disproportionate punishment is the use of private prisons to detain convicted illegal immigrants.

SB 1070 is constructed at every level to govern and regulate the movements of those whom the state of Arizona has deemed to pose a threat to the well-being of its citizenry. This is precisely where the similarities between the Mississippi Black Codes of 1865 and SB 1070 begin to take shape. Although there is a span of 145 years between the passage of the two laws that includes the ratification of the Thirteenth and Fourteenth Amendments to the U.S. Constitution, the passage of numerous Civil Rights Acts, and federal legislation regulating immigration, the state of Arizona empowered itself (seemingly in direct opposition to the Supremacy Clause in Article Six of the U.S. Constitution) to legislate on immigration issues including the status and rights of those who might be legal residents but are suspected of being illegal immigrants. The Mississippi Black Codes and SB 1070 establish a highly regulated system in which to monitor and control blacks and Latina/os, respectively, through broadly worded statutes that make it impossible to enforce the law without constructing suspicion based on racial categories. In addition to this, the perception of black and brown skin is the only consistent measurable factor in establishing probable cause for investigating one's presence. Unlike the legal adage "innocent until proven guilty," in the case of blacks in Mississippi right after the Civil War and Latina/os in contemporary Arizona, the legal system presumes guilty until proven innocent based on skin pigmentation. Both laws criminalized vagrancy, required the maintenance of files on persons within the suspected group, compulsory enforcement by state officials, illegality of aiding suspected persons in anyway, forbidding suspected persons to be in the possession of anything that could be perceived as a threat to the public (including firearms, deadly weapons, and mind-altering substances), and, finally, if one's innocence could not be proven, the imposition of heavy fines, jail terms, and possible indentured servitude through a public and private alliance where the guilty party would be sent to serve their time while simultaneously incurring a continuous debt due to their imprisonment that must be paid off either through monetary payments or work.

The crux of the Mississippi Black Codes and frankly, what could be called Arizona's Brown Codes, is the ontological illegality of black and brown skin in each state. The dichotomy here comes down to the beingness of disputed bodies. In both cases, the society at large and the power structure defined black and brown persons as totally different and antithetical to the maintenance and well-being of society. As with the 1790 Naturalization Act and the debate over who qualified as white at the turn of the twentieth century, Mississippi—and more importantly to this argument, Arizona—set up legislative authority to determine who is a part and subsequently not a part of society through a null hypothesis legal structure. By declaring brown bodies as suspect without a framework for ascertaining probable cause, the enforcement of the law is left to the predilections of societal stereotypes (as in the SCOTUS opinion against Thind) that view Hispanics and Latina/os as beyond the pale of U.S. citizenry. As Mississippi used the Black Codes to solidify white power over blacks through the hyper-enforcement of the myths of blacks as a menace to society, so too Arizona has used the national myths purported by a white power that to be Hispanic or Latina/o makes one a danger to American society. In both cases, whiteness is maintained by making nonwhiteness illegal.

Both of these examples illustrate ways in which the ultimacy of white supremacist Christianity enacts itself for the preservation of white power. In constructing a place of ultimacy through the spatial idea of whiteness, the white supremacist faith acts in whatever manner it must to ensure the continued dominance of whiteness. The passage of the Black and Brown Codes created meaning for whites in Mississippi and Arizona by the maintenance of a system in which whites maintain control culturally, socially, and spiritually. Adherence to the white supremacist faith means ensuring that no others can maintain a "beside-each-otherness" because of the totalizing reality of ultimate meaning. To consent to a power in which whiteness could be subverted by nonwhites calls into question the godliness of white supremacist Christianity. For this reason, societal structures create systems of different degrees of ferocity that ensure that whiteness maintains its dominance. In Arizona and Mississippi, the legal system was used to isolate the threat of brown and black people. Whites used the social order to regulate every action and movement within the system. Any action that could be perceived as a threat to whiteness was deemed illegal in order to place whiteness as the center of society while putting brown and black bodies on the teetering edge between regulated otherness and threat.

CONCLUSION

The dichotomy of whiteness and nonwhiteness solidified itself early in the psyche of the United States with the passage of the first immigration law in 1790 that turned the old world language of Christian and heathen into the modern racialized bifurcation of black and white, and later on other groups and whites. In this way, the precedent was set for the privileges of citizenship to be tied to whiteness. While the classification of whiteness as equal to citizenship has changed in legal terms since 1790, the psychological power of whiteness still presents a powerful commodification of appearance and action. The denial of citizenship to Ozawa and Thind based on their status as nonwhite and non-Christian shows that the legacy of the 1790 law lived well into the twentieth century. The power of "Christianity" and "whiteness" as connected terms shows the inherent theological nature of what it means to be a citizen in the United States. Justice Sutherland could not conceive of a citizenry not defined by the permanent connection of Christian and white.

The permanence of Christianity and whiteness as determinate in the status of citizen also showed itself in the construction of the Black Codes in the South after the Civil War and Arizona's Brown Codes in the twenty-first century. These codes established social parameters in which what is not white is suspect. Vagrancy laws make it possible for whites to legislate the illegal nature of nonwhite bodies in societies while at the same time sanctifying whiteness. To pass as white meant to be free, while not to be white meant to be illegal. In this way, a priesthood was formed that established American society as a place of safety for those belonging to the in-group. This also meant the construction of an out-group based on the absence of whiteness. The soteriology of white flesh dominated the construction of the United States through the definition of citizenship. The image of the white Christ is a representation of the belief in the sacredness of whiteness within American society. As such, the sacred place of whiteness is ensured by eternally connecting it to the freedom of the citizen.

NOTES

1. Emphasis added by the author.

2. An Act to Establish an Uniform Rule of Naturalization, 1st Cong., 2d sess. (March 26, 1790.

3. Richard W. Flourney, Jr., "Naturalization and Expatriation," *The Yale Law Journal* 31, no. 7 (May 1922): 708.

4. The U.S. Congress would eventually settle on a five-year residency requirement, an oath of citizenship, and the renunciation of citizenship in other countries.

5. Elaine A. Robinson, *Race and Theology* (Nashville: Abingdon Press, 2012), 67.

6. See the First Charter of Virginia (1606), the Charter of Carolina (1663), the Charter of Delaware (1701), and the Charter of Georgia (1732).

7. Matthew Frye Jacobson, *Whiteness of a Different Color: European Immigrants and the Alchemy of Race* (Cambridge: Harvard University Press, 1999), 23.

8. Rebecca Anne Goetz, *The Baptism of Early Virginia: How Christianity Created Race* (Baltimore: The Johns Hopkins University Press, 2012), 35.

9. Bartolomé de las Casas,.*In Defense of the Indians*. Trans. and edited by Stafford Poole (Dekalb, IL: Northern Illinois University, 1974), 11.

10. Ibid.

11. Ibid.

12. Howard Zinn, *A People's History of the United States: 1492–Present* (New York: Harper Collins, 2005), 4.

13. In this understanding of Christian, I am referring to Protestantism as it pertains to the theological shift in the symbolism of baptism. As noted earlier, Roman Catholic conceptions of conversion during the colonial period hinged on converting

the indigenous people. Unlike the Roman Catholic approach, Protestants in the United States disassociated the freedom of conversion from the freedom of self. Conversion did not provide a connection to the larger society; rather, these connections were based on the spatial particularities of white supremacist Christianity.

14. Rebecca Anne Goetz, *The Baptism of Early Virginia: How Christianity Created Race* (Baltimore: The John Hopkins University Press, 2012), 111.

15. Sylvester A. Johnson, *The Myth of Ham in Nineteenth-Century American Christianity: Race, Heathens, and the People of God* (New York: Palgrave MacMillan, 2004), 45.

16. Ibid., 4.

17. Ibid.

18. Ibid., 47.

19. Ibid., 47–8.

20. Ibid., 49.

21. Ibid.

22. Eric Weitz, "Nationalism," in *The Oxford Handbook of Holocaust Studies*, edited by Peter Hayes and John K. Roth (New York: Oxford University Press, 2010), 65.

23. Ibid.

24. Johnson, *The Myth of Ham in Nineteenth-Century American Christianity*, 49.

25. Matthew Frye Jacobson, *Whiteness of a Different Color: European Immigrants and the Alchemy of Race* (Cambridge: Harvard University Press, 1999), 28.

26. Ibid., 22.

27. *Ozawa v. United States* and *United States v. Thind* were not the only cases heard before SCOTUS on the "free white persons" clause, but these two cases most aptly demonstrate judicial views on whiteness because of their proximity to each other.

28. Devon W. Carbado, "Yellow by Law" *California Law Review* 97, no. 3 (June 2009): 636.

29. Ibid., 639.

30. Ibid.

31. *Ozawa v. United States*, 260 U.S. 178 (1922).

32. Ibid.

33. Carbado, "Yellow by Law," 653.

34. *Ozawa v. United States*.

35. Ibid.

36. Ibid.

37. Ibid.

38. Ibid.

39. Jennifer Snow, "The Civilization of White Men: The Race of the Hindu in *United States v. Bhagat Singh Thind*," in *Race, Nation, and Religion in the Americas*, edited by Henry Goldschmidt and Elizabeth McAlister (New York: Oxford University Press, 2004), 259.

40. *United States v. Thind*, 261 U.S. 204 (1923).

41. Ibid.

42. Ian Haney López, *White by Law: The Legal Construction of Race* (New York: NYU Press, 2006), 62.

43. Ibid.

44. Ibid.

45. *United States v. Thind*.

46. Ibid.

47. Ibid.

48. Ibid.

49. In this instance, the court is using Hindu as a racial concept, rather than a religious one.

50. Pinn, "Putting Jesus in His Place," *Humanism: Essays on Race, Religion and Popular Culture* (New York: Bloomsbury Academic, 2015), 78.

51. Ibid.

52. Paul Tillich, *Theology of Culture*, edited by Robert C. Kimball (New York: Oxford University Press, 1959), 32.

53. Ibid., 33.

54. Haney López, *White by Law: The Legal Construction of Race*, 56.

55. Ibid., 66.

56. Anthony B. Pinn, "Putting Jesus in His Place," *Humanism: Essays on Race, Religion and Popular Culture* (New York: Bloomsbury Academic, 2015), 79.

57. Haney López, *White by Law: The Legal Construction of Race*, 73.

58. Ibid., 75.

59. John Tehranian, "Performing Whiteness: Naturalization Litigation and the Construction of Racial Identity in America," *The Yale Law Journal* 109, no. 4 (Jan. 2000): 827–8.

60. During the same time period in U.S. history, Roman Catholics and Jews were also considered questionable candidates for citizenship.

61. W.E.B. Du Bois used the idea of the "psychological wage" as a way of demonstrating the ways in which whites, particularly low-income whites, benefited from their whiteness. See W.E.B. Du Bois, *Black Reconstruction in America, 1860–1880* (New York: The Free Press, 1962), 700–1: David R. Roediger expands on Du Bois' idea of the psychological wage in his works on working-class whites and how the framing of whiteness enables them to take pride in at least not being black. See David R. Roediger, *Wages of Whiteness: Race and the Making of the American Working Class*, Rev. ed. (New York: Verso Books, 2007), 12–13.

62. In addition to Mississippi, several other states passed Black Codes in the aftermath of the Civil War that were highly influenced by this legislation, including Alabama, Louisiana, and South Carolina in 1865. In 1866, Arkansas, Florida, Georgia, Kentucky, North Carolina, Tennessee, Texas, and Virginia passed versions of the Black Codes as well. For more information, see John M. Mecklin, "The Black Codes," *The South Atlantic Quarterly* 16, v. 3 (1917): 248–259.

63. Mississippi Black Code, *Laws of the State of Mississippi* (October–December, 1865), 82–93.

64. Ibid.

65. Ibid.

66. Ibid.

67. Ibid.

68. Isabel Wilkerson, *The Warmth of Other Suns: The Epic Story of America's Great Migration* (New York: Vintage Books, 2011), 53–4.

69. Mississippi Black Code, *Laws of the State of Mississippi.*

70. Ibid.

71. Ibid.

72. Ibid. and Goetz, 78.

73. Mississippi Black Code, *Laws of the State of Mississippi.*

74. Ibid.

75. Ibid.

76. Ibid.

77. Ibid.

78. Ibid.

79. Ibid.

80. Nik Theodore, "Policing Borders: Unauthorized Immigration and the Pernicious Politics of Attrition," *Social Justice* 38, no. ½ (2011): 90.

81. Amanda Rose, *Showdown in the Sonoran Desert: Religion, Law and the Immigration Controversy* (New York: Oxford University Press, 2012), 125.

82. Ranchers Alarmed by Killing Near Border, *New York Times*, April 10, 2010, accessed February 13, 2015, http://www.nytimes.com/2010/04/05/us/05arizona.html.

83. The Support Our Law Enforcement and Safe Neighborhoods Act, 49th Legislature, 2nd Regular Session (April 23, 2010).

84. Ibid.

85. Ibid.

Conclusion

On January 20, 2017, Donald Trump took the Oath of Office and officially succeeded Barack Obama as president of the United States. In that moment, the seat of power and the White House returned to a white man. The country witnessed the return of the executive mansion back to white men, who with the exception of Barack Obama had been its occupants for the duration of its history. But is Donald Trump just another white man sitting behind the Resolute Desk? He began his rise as a politician by becoming the most influential supporter of the birther movement, seeking to discredit the legitimacy of Obama. While Trump believes he successfully ended the controversy,[1] he has been taken up as a figurehead by white supremacists (like David Duke, David Spencer, and Milo Yiannopoulos). Trump's adamant support of building a wall along the Mexican border,[2] deporting illegal immigrants,[3] and the banning of persons from certain predominately Muslim countries,[4] and his nomination of an attorney general who was denied a federal judgeship over claims of racism[5] all demonstrate the influence of white supremacist Christianity on shaping the policies of the Trump administration at a conscious or unconscious level.

Based on Trump's actions in office, what is certain is that the power of white supremacist Christianity is not diminishing. In fact, moments of racial progression often lead to a revival of white supremacist support. As the white Christ restores order to the United States as a white republic, are we bound to forget the upheaval rendered in the white consciousness by the presidency of Barack Obama? *The Religion of White Supremacy in the United States* would not be possible without such an upheaval in the white psyche. Donald Trump's charismatic and irreverent persona has enabled whites to express racist attitudes in more blatant ways. This makes the present situation in the United States one of those possible moments of racial regression.

This book shows that while many whites think that race is no longer an issue in the United States, the country's history says otherwise. When we understand white supremacy as a religion, we can see how the ultimacy of white flesh shapes lived reality in America. This work was built upon the increased open actions of white supremacy during the Obama years to answer how a country claiming colorblindness showed a different story with a non-white person trespassing on white space of the White House.

This work demonstrates that white supremacy is a religion in the United States, but it will take the work of others to continue to connect the work of Critical Whiteness Studies to Religious Studies and Theology. While some works have started this conversation, many more scholars will have to add their expertise to this endeavor. Deconstructing the powers of white supremacy cannot be left only to nonwhite scholars. This is a necessary place for whites to call out, deconstruct, and investigate a system that they live within. The reality of white supremacy is that whites who study it are also living their lives within a system that they cannot honestly escape from. And yet, the study of racism and religion has for far too long been left to minority scholars. This trend must change.

The Religion of White Supremacy in the United States focused only on small aspects within the formulation of white supremacy as a religion as a way to start a much longer and long-overdue conversation. To start, this work had to leave the context of the United States or even British theological systems to comprehend how white supremacy became a powerful system of operation within this nation. The Spanish debates about the humanness of the people found in the Americas showed a crisis of understanding. There was evidence of people West of the Atlantic Ocean, but the existence of whole civilizations there forced the people of Europe to reshape their understanding of world. This new understanding became the beginning of the white supremacy that would eventually form in the United States and would also seek control of the rest of the world. The use of Christian theology to shape how the people of the Americas became heathen set in motion a new relationship between the people of what would be known as Europe and the rest of the world.

Moving to the American shores, the people who were at once Christian and British had formed a much stronger view of their place in the world and their connection to God through theological superiority. As with the Spanish, these theologies became even more important once the British encountered the indigenous people. The Puritan belief in their chosenness as God's people had to guide at every instance to ensure their place in the New World. This chosenness became imperative with the continued expansion of the Mas-sachusetts Bay Colony into Pequot territory. The contentious relationship forced the Puritans to understand their connection to God in new ways. The formation of the epistemology of whiteness assured the white people of their place as God's chosen people and justified the removal of the Pequot people. The horrific events at Fort Mystic instilled the divine power of God as exclusively connected to the white Puritans. The references to the glory of God in accounts of the massacre would continue with the people of God in constructing a white nation.

The founding of the white nation in 1789 led to the next important step where the people of the nation viewed it as white space. The Naturalization Act of 1790 took the belief of God's chosen people and legislated it into the very fabric of the country. Thenceforth, to become a citizen of the new nation, one had to be *white*. This completely changed the dynamics between citizen and noncitizen. From this point forward, to be white afforded an exclusionary place within the body politic that gave an insurmountable amount of power to those classified as white. From this powerful moment in U.S. history, the idea of whiteness became not just a belief, but a way of life: a white supremacist life.

The formation of white space by the Naturalization Act of 1790 took white supremacy to the next level. Officially, the United States became a country in which participation would be predicated on being white. President Andrew Jackson lived out this power of the white nation by expanding white space from the specialness of whiteness to the specialness of American space as constructed for whites only. He understood the world through the power of white supremacy. The physical land, in addition to the people, became special. The white nation could no longer accept the placement of heathen bodies, as represented by the Five Civilized Nations, within white America. The presence of the five nations contradicted the specialness of America and its relationship with the white God.

The dynamics of specialness and space would continue to determine the place of America in the world. Andrew Jackson's religion of white supremacy moved forward for the next century solidifying its place within the United States, and yet the twentieth century would bring significant questions to the place of the white God. With the Tulsa Race Riot and the Supreme Court cases *Ozawa* and *Thind*, the United States faced a moment in which the ultimacy of white supremacy had to reinforce itself within the culture and society. All were moments where the power of white supremacy had to be defended to protect the honor of the white God. Tulsa was a moment in history where the extralegal powers of white supremacy could have started to fade. The denial of a lynching was a serious impingement upon the relationship between the white God and its people. To not fight this injustice to the white God would be anathema to the faith. The people of God had to show that Tulsa was white space. This meant the destruction of the black space that was an abomination to the religion of white supremacy.

The cases of *Ozawa* and *Thind* were arguably more important to the reassertion of the ultimacy of white supremacy in the United States. For the Court to rule in favor of either man would have destroyed the sacred foundations of the United States as a white nation. More importantly, these cases showed that the rule of law was subservient to the ultimacy of white supremacy. In less than four months, the Court had to completely reject its own line of thinking. Ultimately, in the making of the *Thind* decision, the Court found the power of whiteness to be beyond the scope of change. The white God demanded obedience from the Court and it obliged in spectacular fashion by ignoring its own legal precedent established only months earlier in *Ozawa*.

A decade after Tulsa, the city of Marion affirmed its commitment to the white God by lynching two black men. The fact of this lynching having taken place so late in history in a northern state contradicts the idea that the religion of white supremacy was limited to the American South after the Civil War. In addition to this, the lynching demonstrated the power of the white community. The people of Marion took pride in participating in an American ritual, and the photograph of the lynching is nothing less than the joyous commemoration of that ritual. The people of the photograph sought the lynching event as a revival of their connection to the white God.

One can move even farther north to Detroit a decade later to witness the power of white space in the legalized segregation of the city. The construction of the wall was a physical representation of the threat black space posed to white space. The necessity of a barrier in this context proved the continued ultimacy of whiteness by seeking to keep blackness separate from the holiness of white flesh. By this point, whites saw blackness as disease to the purity of whiteness, a plague to the white nation that must be quarantined from God's people.

The final pieces of historical evidence—like the issues surrounding the use of the Redskins emblem by the NFL team in Washington, D.C.—bring the history of the religion of white supremacy into the contemporary moment. With the use of the name and emblem, the Washington Redskins fulfill two powerful acts of white supremacy. First, the team is continuing the legacy of the divine right of white space in the white nation. The team owner does not recognize the issue of the Redskins name and emblem as markers of genocide, and yet, it is hard to deny the continued honoring of white power in the mythical nature of its use. Secondly, the team is honoring the identity of the nation by using the name and emblem by pointing to the revolutionary ideals of liberty and freedom instilled in the white imaginary. Both perspectives leave the place of Indianness at the mercy of white supremacy by making the place of indigenous people contingent on play within white space rather than of its own accord.

Finally, Arizona's passage of SB 1070 to limit the movement of brown bodies in white space bears more than a passing similarity to the Black Codes passed in Mississippi after the Civil War. Arizona's Brown Codes make illegal the movement of brown bodies within white space. The marking of brown bodies as inherently illegal mirrors the attitude of the early twentieth-century Supreme Court when it reasoned that a "Hindu" man could never be a citizen. The preservation of the white nation means that nonwhite bodies must forever be seen as suspicious within the United States. Any other option would call into question the power of the white God through the diminishment of the ultimacy of white supremacy in the American psyche. This would cause a split personality in a nation founded not on the premise of liberty but on the superiority of white space.

This history brings the religion of white supremacy back to the image of the white Christ. While Sallman and later his representatives see *Head of Christ* as a depiction of the Messiah, this Christ image is also the personification of a much larger theological history that would make it impossible for the Christian savior to be anything but white. Even in attempts to change the historical color of Christ, what is lost is that the white Christ represents so much more than paint and brushstrokes. The identity of the white Christ is located not on canvas but in the psyche of white America. This is not changed by paint color. The religion of white supremacy is the manifestation of the ultimacy found within the salvific nature white flesh brings to God's chosen people. The ultimacy of white supremacy is symbolized in Sallman work, but its theological reality lies in the everyday working of white supremacy as it asserts itself in the preservation of white space.

NOTES

1. Melanie Mason, "Donald Trump did not put an end to the 'Birther' Controversy in 2011, Despite His Claims to the Contrary," *Los Angeles Times*, September 26, 2016, http://www.politico.com/story/2016/09/donald-trump-stop-and-frisk-228486.

2. Exec. Order: Border Security and Immigration Enforcement Improvements (January 25, 2017), https://www.whitehouse.gov/the-press-office/2017/01/25/executive-order-border-security-and-immigration-enforcement-improvements.

3. Exec. Order: Enhancing Public Safety in the Interior of the United States (January 25, 2017), https://www.whitehouse.gov/the-press-office/2017/01/25/presidential-executive-order-enhancing-public-safety-interior-united.

4. Exec. Order: Protecting the Nation from Foreign Terrorist Entry into the United States (January 27, 2017), https://www.whitehouse.gov/the-press-office/2017/01/27/executive-order-protecting-nation-foreign-terrorist-entry-united-states.

5. Amber Phillips, "That Time the Senate Denied Jeff Sessions a Federal Judgeship Over Accusations of Racism," *Washington Post*, January 10, 2017, https://www.washingtonpost.com/news/the-fix/wp/2016/11/18/that-time-the-senate-denied-jeff-sessions-a-federal-judgeship-over-accusations-of-racism/?utm_term=.e412d504abb4.

Bibliography

Agamben, Giorgio. *Homo Sacer: Sovereign Power and Bare Life*. Translated by Daniel Heller-Roazen. Stanford, CA: Stanford University Press, 1998.

Ahn, Ilsup, Agnes Chiu, and William O'Neill. "'And You Welcomed Me?': A Theological Response to the Militarization of Undocumented Immigrants." *Crosscurrents* (September 2013): 303–322.

Albrecht, Gloria. "Detroit: Still the 'Other' America." *Journal of the Society of Christian Ethics* 29, no. 1 (Spring/Summer 2009): 2–23.

Avery, Burnice. *Walk Quietly Through the Night and Cry Softly*. Detroit: Balamp Publishing, 1977.

Bailey, Richard A. *Race and Redemption in Puritan New England*. New York: Oxofrd University Press, 2011.

Baker, Kelly J. *Gospel According to the Klan: The KKK's Appeal to Protestant America, 1915–1930*. Lawrence: University Press of Kansas, 2011.

Baldwin, James. *The Fire Next Time*. New York: Vintage Books, 1993.

Bell, Derrick A. *Faces at the Bottom of the Well: The Permanence of Racism*. New York, NY: Basic Books, 1992.

Bergen, Doris L. *War and Genocide: A Concise History of the Holocaust*. New York: Rowman & Littlefield Publishers, Inc., 2003.

Blum, Edward J. *Reforging the White Republic: Race, Religion and American Nationalism, 1865–1898*. Baton Rouge, LA: Louisiana State University Press, 2005.

———. *W.E.B. Du Bois: American Prophet*. Philadelphia: University of Pennsylvania of Press, 2009.

Blum, Edward J, and Paul Harvey. *The Color of Christ: The Son of God and the Saga of Race in America*. Chapel Hill: The University of North Carolina Press, 2012.

Bonilla-Silva, Eduardo. *Racism Without Racists: Color-Blind Racism and Racial Inequality in Contemporary America*. Third Edition. New York: Rowman & Littlefield Publishers, Inc., 2010.

Brophy, Alfred L. *Reconstructing the Dreamland: The Tulsa Race Riot of 1921 Race, Reparations, and Reconciliation*. New York: Oxford University Press, 2002.

Brown, Hana E. "Race, Legality, and the Social Policy Consequences of Anti-Immigration Mobilization." *American Sociological Review* 78, no. 2 (2013): 290–314.

Brown, D. Mackenzie. *Ultimate Concern: Tillich in Dialogue*. New York: Harper and Row Publishers, 1965.

Buckser, Andrew S. "Lynching as Ritual in the American South." *Berkeley Journal of Sociology* 37 (1992): 11–28.

Burnstein, William. *The Logic of Evil: The Social Origins of the Nazi Party, 1925–1933*. New Haven, CT: Yale University Press, 1996.

Cannon, Katie Geneva, Emilie M. Townes, and Angela D. Sims, ed. *Womanist Theological Ethics: A Reader*. Louisville, KY: Westminster John Know Press, 2011.

Carbado, Devon W. "Yellow by Law." *California Law Review* 97, no. 3 (June 2009): 633–692.

Carroll, James. *Constantine's Sword: The Church and the Jews*. New York: Mariner Books, 2002.

Carter, J. Kameron. *Race: A Theological Account*. New York: Oxford University Press, 2008.

Cave, Alfred A. *The Pequot War*. Amherst, MA: University of Massachusetts Press, 1996.

Cecelski, David S, and Timothy B. Tyson, ed. *Democracy Betrayed: The Wilington Race Riot of 1898 and Its Legacy*. Chapel Hill, NC: The University of North Carolina Press, 1998.

Coates, Ta-Nehisi. "The Case for Reparations." *Atlantic*, June 2014. Accessed March 3, 2015. http://www.theatlantic.com/features/archive/2014/05/the-case-for-reparations/361631/.

Columbus, Christopher. *The Four Voyages of Christopher Columbus*, ed. and trans. by J.M. Cohen. New York: Penguin Books, 1969.

Clotfeller, Charles T. "The Detroit Decision and 'White Flight.'" *The Journal of Legal Studies* 5, no. 1 (January 1976): 99–112.

Cone, James H. *The Cross and the Lynching Tree*. Maryknoll, NY: Orbis Books, 2011.

Cruz, Eduardo R. "The Demonic for the Twenty-first Century." *Currents in Theology and Mission* 28 (2001): 420–428.

Daines, Marvel. *Be It So Ever Tumbled: The Story of a Suburban Slum*. Citizen's Housing and Planning Council of Detroit, March 1940.

Debo, Angie. *A History of the Indians of the United States*. Norman: University of Oklahoma Press, 1984.

De La Torre, Miguel A, and Stacey M. Floyd-Thomas, ed. *Beyond the Pale: Reading Theology from the Margins*. Louisville, KY: Westminster John Know Press, 2011.

Delgado, Richard, and Jean Stefancic. *Critical Race Theory: An Introduction*. 2nd ed. New York: New York University Press, 2012.

Deloria, Philip J. *Playing Indian*. New Haven: Yale University Press, 1998.

Douglas, Kelly Brown. *The Black Christ*. Maryknoll, NY: Orbis Books, 1994.

———. *Stand Your Ground: Black Bodies and the Justice of God*. Maryknoll, NY: Orbis Books, 2015.

Du Bois, W.E.B. *Darkwater Voices From Within the Veil*. Mineola, NY: Dover Publications, Inc., 1999.

———. *Dusk of Dawn: An Essay Toward an Autobiography of a Race Concept*. New Brunswick: Transaction Publishers, 1995.

———. *Black Reconstruction in America, 1860–1880*. New York: The Free Press, 1962.

———. *The Souls of Black Folk*. New York: Barnes & Noble Classics, 2003.

Dussel, Enrique. *Ethics of Liberation: In the Age of Globalization and Exclusion*. Translated by Eduardo Mendieta. Durham: Duke University Press, 2013.

———. *Invention of the Americas: Eclipse of "the Other" and the Myth of Modernity*. Translated by Michael B. Barber. New York: Continuum, 1995.

———. *Politics of Liberation: A Critical Global History*. Translated by Thia Cooper. New York: SCM Press, 2011.

Ellsworth, Scott. *Death in a Promised Land: The Tulsa Race Riot of 1921*. Baton Rouge, LA: Louisiana State University Press, 1982.

Flourney, Jr., Richard W. "Naturalization and Expatriation." *The Yale Law Journal* 31, no. 7 (May 1922): 702–719.

Foucault, Michel. *The Birth of Biopolitics: Lectures at the Collège de France, 1978–1979*. Edited by Michel Senellart. Translated by Graham Burchell. New York: Picador, 2008.

———. *The History of Sexuality: An Introduction, Volume 1*. Translated by Robert Hurley. New York: Vintage Books, 1990.

Frederickson, George M. *The Black Image in the White Mind: The Debate on Afro-American Character and Destiny, 1817–1914*. New York: Harper & Row, 1971.

———. *Racism: A Short History*. Princeton, NJ: Princeton University Press, 2002.

Goetz, Rebecca Anne. *The Baptism of Early Virginia: How Christianity Created Race*. Baltimore: The John Hopkins University Press, 2012.

Gossett, Thomas F. *Race: The History of An Idea in America*. New York: Oxford University Press, 1997.

Halliburton, Jr., R. "The Tulsa Race War of 1921." *Journal of Black Studies* 2, no. 3 (March 1972): 333–357.

Handy, Robert T. "The American Messianic Consciousness: The Concept of the Chosen People and Manifest Destiny." *Review and Expositor* 73, no. 1 (Winter 1976): 47–58.

Hanke, Lewis. *All Mankind is One: A Study of the Disputation Between Bartolomé de las Casas and Juan Ginés de Sepúlveda in 1550 on the Religious and Intellectual Capacity of the American Indians*. Dekalb, IL: Northern Illinois University Press, 1994.

Harris, Cheryl I. "Whiteness as Property." *Harvard Law Review* 106, no. 8 (June 1993): 1707–1791.

Hayes, Peter, and John K. Roth, eds. *The Oxford Handbook of Holocaust Studies*. New York: Oxford University Press, 2010.

Hemmer, Jr., Joseph J. "Exploitation of American Indian Symbols: A First Amendment Analysis." *American Indian Quarterly* 32, no. 2 (Spring 2008): 121–140.

Higham, John. *Strangers in the Land: Patterns of American Nativism 1860–1925.* Westport, CT: Greenwood Press, Publishers, 1980.

Hirsch, James S. *Riot and Remembrance: America's Worst Race Riot and Its Legacy.* New York: Mariner Books, 2002.

Hofmann, Sudie. "The Elimination of Indigenous Mascots, Logos, and Nicknames: Organizing on College Campuses." *American Indian Quarterly* 29, nos. 1&2 (Winter & Spring 2005): 156–177.

Hubbard, William. *A Narrative of the Indian Wars in New-England.* Boston: John Boyle in Marlborough Street, 1775.

Jacobson, Matthew Frye. *Whiteness of a Different Color: European Immigrants and the Alchemy of Race.* Cambridge: Harvard University Press, 1999.

Jennings, Willie James. *The Christian Imagination: Theology and the Origins of Race.* New Haven: Yale University Press, 2011.

Johnson, Daniel Morley. "From the Tomahawk Chop to the Road Block: Discourses of Savagism in Whitestream Media." *American Indian Quarterly* 35, no. 1 (Winter 2011): 104–134.

Johnson, Wayne G. "Martin Luther's Law-Gospel Distinction and Paul Tillich's Method of Correlation: a Study in Parallels." *The Lutheran Quarterly* 23 (1971): 274–288.

Johnson, Sylvester A. *The Myth of Ham in Nineteenth-Century American Christianity: Race, Heathenism, and the People of God.* New York: Palgrave MacMillan, 2004.

Jones, William R. *Is God a White Racist: A Preamble to Black Theology.* Boston: Beacon Press, 1997.

Kelsey, George D. *Racism and the Christian Understanding of Man.* New York: Charles Scribner's Sons, 1965.

King, C. Richard. "Looking Back to a Future End: Reflections on the Symposium on Racist Stereotypes in American Sport at the National Museum of the American Indian." *American Indian Quarterly* 38, no. 2 (Spring 2014): 135–142.

King, C. Richard, and Charles Frueling Springwood, eds. *Beyond the Cheers: Race as Spectacle in College Sport.* Albany: State University of New York Press, 2001.

———. *Team Spirits: The Native American Mascots Controversy.* Lincoln: University of Nebraska Press, 2001.

King, Jr., Martin Luther. *Why We Can't Wait.* Boston: Beacon Press, 1986.

Knoll, Benjamin R. "'And Who Is My Neighbor?' Religion and Immigration Policy Attitudes." *Journal for the Scientific Study of Religion* 48, no. 2 (2009): 313–331.

Kunnie, Julian. "Apartheid in Arizona: HB 2281 and Arizona's Denial of Human Rights of Peoples of Color" *The Black Scholar* 40, no. 4 (Winter 2010): 16–26.

Las Casas, Bartolomé de. *In Defense of the Indians.* Translated and Edited by Stafford Poole. Dekalb, IL: Northern Illinois University, 1974.

Lee, Linda, ed. *A New Dawn in Beloved Community: Stories with the Power to Transform.* Nashville: Abingdon Press, 2012.

Lewis, Douglass. "The Conceptual Structure of Tillich's Method of Correlation." *Encounter* 28 (1967): 263–274.

Lipsitz, George. *The Possessive Investment in Whiteness: How White People Profit From Identity Politics.* Philadelphia: Temple University Press, 1998.

Loewen, James W. *Sundown Towns: A Hidden Dimension of American Racism*. New York: New Press, 2005.

López, Ian Haney. *White by Law: The Legal Construction of Race*. New York: New York University Press, 2006.

Losada, Angel. "The Controversy Between Sepulveda and Las Casas in the Junta of Valladolid." In *Bartolomé de las Casas in History: Toward an Understanding of the Man and His Work*, 278–307, edited by Juan Friede and Benjamin Keen. Dekalb: Northern Illinois University, 1971.

MacIntosh, Peggy. "White Privilege: Unpacking the Invisible Knapsack." In *White Privilege: Essential Readings on the Other Side of Racism*, 3rd edition, 123–128, edited by Paula S. Rothenberg. New York: Worth Publishers, 2008.

Madison, James H. *A Lynching in the Heartland: Race and memory in America*. New York: Palgrave MacMillan, 2001.

Mallow, Vernon R. *The Demonic: A Selected Theological Study: An Examination into the Theology of Edwin Lewis, Karl Barth, and Paul Tillich*. New York: University Press of America, 1983.

Martines, George A. "Immigration and the Meaning of United States Citizenship: Whiteness and Assimilation." *Washburn Law Journal* 46: 335–344.

Mason, John. *Major Mason's Brief History of the Pequot War*. Boston: S. Kneeland & T. Green in Queen-Street, 1736.

McGrath, Alister. *Christian Theology: An Introduction*, 3rd Edition. New York: Blackwell Publishing, 2001.

McKoy, Sheila Smith. *When Whites Riot: Writing Race and Violence in American and South African Culture*. Madison: University of Wisconsin Press, 2001.

Messer, Chris M, "The Tulsa Race Riot of 1921: Toward and Integrative Theory of Collective Violence." *Journal of Social History* 44, no. 4 (Summer 2011): 1217–1232.

Messer, Chris M. and Patricia A. Bell. "Mass Media and Governmental Framing of Riots: The Case of Tulsa, 1921." *Journal of Black Studies* 40, no. 5 (May 2010): 851–870.

Mignolo, Walter D. *The Darker Side of Western Modernity: Global Futures, Decolonial Options*. Durham: Duke University Press, 2011.

Mills, Charles W. *The Racial Contract*. Ithaca, NY: Cornell University Press, 1997.

———. "Revisionist Ontologies: Theorizing White Supremacy." *Social and Economic Studies* 43, no. 3 (September 1994): 105–134.

Moore, MariJo, eds. *Genocide of the Mind: New Native American Writing*. New York: Thunder's Mouth Press/Nation Books, 2003.

Morgan, David. "Sallman's *Head of Christ*: The History of an Image." *The Christian Century*, October 7, 1992.

Morrison, Toni. *The Bluest Eye*. New York: Alfred A. Knopf, 2000.

Muhammad, Ismail. "The 1921 Tulsa Race Riot." *Los Angeles Sentinel* 77, no. 26 (2011).

Newport, John P. *Paul Tillich*. Peabody, MA: Hendrickson Publishers, 1984.

Plaskow, Judith. *Sex, Sin and Grace: Women's Experience and the Theologies of Reinhold Niebuhr and Paul Tillich*. New York: University Press of America, 1980.

Perkinson, James W. *White Theology: Outing Supremacy in Modernity*. New York: Palgrave MacMillan, 2004.

Peterseim, Locke. "Not Just Whistling Dixie in D.C." *ESPN*. Accessed on February 22, 2015, http://espn.go.com/page2/wash/s/closer/020315.html.

Prothero, Stephen. *The American Jesus: How the Son of God Became A National Icon*. New York: Farrar, Straus, and Giroux, 2003.

Prucha, Francis Paul, ed. *Documents of United States Indian Policy*. Lincoln: University of Nebraska Press, 1990.

Raper, Arthur F. *The Tragedy of Lynching*. Chapel Hill: The University of North Carolina Press, 1933.

Ray Jr., Stephen G. "An Unintended Conversation Partner: Tillich's Account of the Demonic and Critical Race Theory." *International Yearbook of Tillich Research* (2014): 63–78.

———. "Contending for the Cross: Black Theology and the Ghosts of Modernity." *Black Theology* 8, no. 1 (2010): 53–68.

———. *Do No Harm: Social Sin and Christian Responsibility*. Minneapolis: Fortress Press, 2003.

Rittenhouse, Bruce P. *Shopping for Meaningful Lives: The Religious Motive of Consumerism*. Eugene, OR: Cascade Books, 2013.

Rivera, Luis N. *A Violent Evangelism: The Political and Religious Conquest of the Americas*. Louisville: Westminster John Knox Press, 1992

Robinson, Elaine A. *Race and Theology*. Nashville: Abingdon Press, 2012.

Rose, Amanda. *Showdown in the Sonoran Desert: Religion, Law and the Immigration Controversy*. New York: Oxford University Press, 2012.

Stewart, III., Carlyle Fielding. "The Method of Correlation in the Theology of James H. Cone." *The Journal of Religious Thought* 40 (1983): 27–38.

Sims, Angela D. *Ethical Complications of Lynching: Ida B. Wells's Interrogation of American Terror*. New York: Palgrave MacMillan, 2010.

———. "The Issue of Race and Lynching." In *Womanist Theological Ethics: A Reader*, 203–216, edited by Katie Geneva Cannon, Emilie M. Townes, and Angela D. Sims. Louisville: Westminster John Knox Press, 2011.

———. "Nooses in Public Spaces: A Womanist Critique of Lynching—21st Century Ethical Dilemma." *The Journal of the Society of Christian Ethics* 29, no. 2 (Fall/Winter 2009): 81–95.

Slater, Peter. "Dynamic Religion, Formative Culture, and the Demonic in History." *Harvard Theological Review* 1 (1999): 95–110.

Snow, Jennifer. "The Civilization of White Men: The Race of the Hindu in *United States v. Bhagat Singh Thind*." *Race, Nation, and Religion in the Americas*, edited by Henry Goldschmidt and Elizabeth McAlister, 259–280. New York: Oxford University Press, 2004.

Spindel, Carol. *Dancing at Halftime: Sports and the Controversy Over American Indian Mascots*. New York: New York University Press, 2000.

Sugrue, Thomas J. *The Origins of the Urban Crisis: Race and Inequality in Postwar Detroit*. Princeton: Princeton University Press, 2005.

Teel, Karen. *Racism and the Image of God*. New York: Palgrave MacMillan, 2010.

Tehranian, John. "Performing Whiteness: Naturalization Litigation and the Construction of Racial Identity in America." *The Yale Law Review* 109, no. 4 (Jan. 2000): 817–848.

Tesler, Michael, and David Sears. *Obama's Race: The 2008 Election and the Dream of a Post-Racial America.* Chicago: University of Chicago Press, 2010.

Thandeka. *Learning to be White: Money, Race, and God in America.* New York: Continuum, 2007.

Theodore, Nik. "Policing Borders: Unauthorized Immigration and The Pernicious Politics of Attrition." *Social Justice* 38, no. 1/2 (2011): 90–106.

Tillich, Paul. *Against the Third Reich: Paul Tillich's Wartime Radio Broadcasts into Nazi Germany.* Edited by Ronald H. Stone and Matthew Lon Weaver. Translated by Matthew Lon Weaver. Louisville, KY: Westminster John Know Press, 1998.

———. *The Courage to Be.* New Haven, CT: Yale University Press, 1953.

———. *Dynamics of Faith.* New York: Perennial Classics, 2001.

———. *The Interpretation of History.* Translated by N.A. Rasetzki and Elsa L. Talmey. New York: Charles Scribner's Sons, 1936.

———. *Love, Power, and Justice: Ontological Analyses and Ethical Applications.* New York: Oxford University Press, 1954.

———. *On the Boundary: An Autobiographical Sketch.* New York: Charles Scribner's Sons, 1966.

———. *Paul Tillich: Theologian of the Boundaries.* Edited by Mark Kline Taylor. San Francisco: Collins Publishers, 1987.

———. *The Socialist Decision.* Translated by Franklin Sherman. New York: Harper and Row Publishers, 1977.

———. *Systematic Theology, Vol. 1.* Chicago: The University of Chicago Press, 1951.

———. *Systematic Theology, Vol. 2.* Chicago: The University of Chicago Press, 1957.

———. *Systematic Theology, Vol. 3.* Chicago: The University of Chicago Press, 1963.

———. *Theology of Culture.* Edited by Robert C. Kimball. New York: Oxford University Press, 1959.

Todorv, Tzvetan. *The Conquest of America: The Question of the Other.* Translated by Richard Howard. New York: Harper & Row, 1984.

Tran, Jonathan. "The New Black Theology." *Christian Century.* February 8, 2012.

Underhill, John. *Newes From America; or, A New and Experimentall Discoverie of New England.* London: F.D., 1638.

Vincent, Phillip. *A True Relation of the Late Battell Fought in New England between the English and the Pequet Salvages.* London: M.P., 1638.

Wallace, Anthony F.C. *The Long, Bitter Trail: Andrew Jackson and the Indians.* New York: Hill and Wang, 1993.

West, Cornel. *Prophesy Deliverance: An Afro-American Revolutionary Christianity.* Philadelphia: The Westminster Press, 1982.

Wilkerson, Isabel. *The Warmth of Other Suns: The Epic Story of America's Great Migration.* New York: Vintage Books, 2011.

Wood, Amy Louise. *Lynching and Spectacle: Witnessing Racial Violence in America, 1890–1940*. Chapel Hill: The University of North Carolina Press, 2009.

Yancy, George. *Black Bodies, White Gazes: The Continuing Significance of Race*. New York: Rowman & Littlefield Publishers, 2008.

———, ed. *Christology and Whiteness: What Would Jesus Do?* New York: Routledge, 2012.

———. *Look, A White!: Philosophical Essays on Whiteness*. Philadelphia: Temple University Press, 2012.

———, ed. *What White Looks Like: African-American Philosophers on the Whiteness Question*. New York: Routledge, 2004.

———. "Whiteness and the Return of the Black Body." *The Journal of Speculative Philosophy* 19, no. 4 (2005): 215–241.

Yip, Francis Ching Wah. *Capitalism as Religion?: A Study of Paul Tillich's Interpretation of Modernity*. Cambridge, MA: Harvard University Press, 2010.

Young, Harvey. "The Black Body as Souvenir in American Lynching." *Theatre Journal* 57 (2005): 639–657.

Ziemer, Gregor. *Education for Death: The Making of the Nazi*. New York: Oxford University Press, 1941.

Zinn, Howard. *A People's History of the United States*. New York: Harper Collins, 2010.

Index

About the Author

Eric A. Weed holds a PhD from Garrett-Evangelical Theological Seminary in Evanston, IL, with a specialization in theological, ethical, and historical studies in 2015. His research concentrates on the intersections of race, religion, and culture.

DISCARD